George Somers Bellamy

Essays from Shakspere

George Somers Bellamy

Essays from Shakspere

ISBN/EAN: 9783744665551

Printed in Europe, USA, Canada, Australia, Japan

Cover: Foto ©Thomas Meinert / pixelio.de

More available books at **www.hansebooks.com**

ESSAYS FROM SHAKSPERE.

ESSAYS FROM SHAKSPERE

BY

SOMERS BELLAMY,

AUTHOR OF "THE NEW SHAKSPERIAN DICTIONARY OF QUOTATIONS,"
"TWO WEDDING RINGS," ETC.

"When goodwill is show'd, though it come too short,
The actor may plead pardon."
                        ANTONY AND CLEOPATRA.

EDINBURGH:
THE EDINBURGH PUBLISHING COMPANY.
LONDON: SIMPKIN, MARSHALL, & CO.

1879.

PREFACE.

As "brevity is the soul of wit," so the brevity of a preface is, only too often, its only merit. Neither directly nor indirectly shall I here attempt to praise or depreciate my work, but leave both in the hands of the critics, from whom I know, by past experience, I may expect justice, if not mercy. In writing these essays I have struggled to keep myself, as far as it was humanly possible, in the background, or altogether out of sight; I have struggled to avoid even the appearance of setting myself up as a teacher, and tried hard to shun the dogmatism so offensive to thinking men and women of to-day. As a lover of Shakspere I yield to none. Few men, with the necessity of having to work for daily bread, have devoted more time and labour to the study of

Shakspere's works than I have; and only as a lover have I here endeavoured to expound and elaborate what I believe to have been the great man's views on the subjects forming this book—with what success remains for the public and the guardians of the public taste now to determine. Should failure attend the work, I know the fault will be wholly mine; and if success, like a true lover I shall place the laurel at the feet of my idol.

37 ASHCHURCH PARK VILLAS,
    SHEPHERD'S BUSH.

CONTENTS.

ESSAY	PAGE
I. MOURNING FOR THE DEAD,	9
II. PLAYS AND PLAYWRIGHTS,	21
III. FAME,	35
IV. SUPERSTITION,	46
V. EDUCATION,	61
VI. WOMAN'S OBEDIENCE,	74
VII. HOPE,	85
VIII. EXPERIENCE,	98
IX. TEMPTATION,	112
X. PUBLIC OPINION,	122
XI. MERCY,	135
XII. PERSEVERANCE,	144
XIII. CONSISTENCY,	153
XIV. DRUNKENNESS,	168
XV. LOVE,	185
XVI. HYPOCRISY,	205
XVII. LOVE OF WEALTH,	216
XVIII. FRIENDSHIP,	227

ESSAYS FROM SHAKSPERE.

Essay I.

MOURNING FOR THE DEAD.

Fool: Good madonna, give me leave to prove you a fool.
Oliv.: Can you do it?
Fool: Dexterously, good madonna.
Oliv.: Make your proof.
Fool: I must catechise you for it, madonna: good my mouse of virtue, answer me.
Oliv.: Well, sir, for want of other idleness, I'll bide your proof.
Fool: Good madonna, why mourn'st thou?
Oliv.: Good fool, for my brother's death.
Fool: I think his soul is in hell, madonna.
Oliv.: I know his soul is in heaven, fool.
Fool: The more fool you, madonna, to mourn for your brother's soul being in heaven.—Take away the fool, gentlemen.

Twelfth Night, Act i. sc. 5.

"To persevere
In obstinate condolement is a course
Of impious stubbornness : 'tis unmanly grief;
It shows a will most incorrect to heaven,
A heart unfortified, a mind impatient,
An understanding simple and unschool'd.
. . . . . .
'Tis a fault to heaven,
A fault against the dead, a fault to nature,
To reason most absurd."

Hamlet, Act i. sc. 2.

THE Rev. A. G. L'Estrange, in a recent work entitled *English Humour*, gives an interesting account of minstrels and fools of the Middle Ages. According to this writer, the Court fool was sometimes a mere idiot and butt, or that he corresponded with his name in having some mental weakness or eccentricity; but it not unfrequently happened that he was a man of genius, far superior to his masters. Taking our Middle Age dramatists as authorities on this subject, it is evident that many of the Court fools were shrewd, clever men, and not unfrequently men of genius. If our dramatists are to be taken alone as authorities on this subject, it would seem that the mere idiot, or man with a mental weakness, was the exception, not the rule; but then considerable allowance must be made for the fact that for dramatic purposes a mere idiot would be useless.

Shakspere's fools are all more or less clever, full of sapient or shrewd remarks, ever getting the best of it in a wordy battle, and often by their observations proving themselves to be, if not always men of genius, certainly superior to their masters.

Their folly is not buffoonery, their pleasantry never inane; they never open their mouths but they pour forth pearls of wisdom, and only, too frequently, for swine to tread upon.

The only fool of whom Shakspere has given us a portrait, who may be said to have something akin to the idiot in his composition, is the fool in *King Lear*, and he shows his foolishness more by action and implied action than by his remarks. It is here worthy of notice that, in giving the names and conditions of the *dramatis personæ* in his various plays, Shakspere has, with the exception of the fool in *King Lear*, called this individual either clown or jester, thus tending to demonstrate, I think, my assertion, that this fool is the only one who may be said to have a mental weakness; and this, I repeat, is shown rather by action than by words. He is a counterpart of King James, who never said a foolish thing and never did a wise one. He points out his master's folly in parting with his kingdom, and roundly terms him fool for so doing : hence he shows his wisdom. But he follows even unto death this foolish master: herein he shows his affection, his faithfulness, his large heart and his little brain. To our text.

The clown in *Twelfth Night,* in the words I have quoted, deals a most absolutely crushing, because logical, blow at the folly of mourning for the dead—a folly to which we are all, or nearly all, addicted ; a folly above which only the superior mind can raise itself. To say as much is to fly audaciously in the face of a wide-spread prejudice. I know it; but though this folly be a universal fact, it cannot lessen the greatness of the folly; for the fact of its folly, its puerility, its impiety, its gross selfishness, remains.

Selfishness! This is the key to the whole secret. It is the key that unlocks the secret drawer of every action. Pure, disinterested action never existed. At the bottom of all action, good or evil, lurks the devil, Self—self-aggrandisement, self-glory, self-praise, if not praise from others: love! the grand passion, the anticipation of joy for self—remove from the lover the physical possibility of the enjoyment he anticipates, and then analyse his love: benevolence! mostly, and at the worst, a mere sprat to catch a whale; rarely, and at the best, the creating of a feeling of *self*-complacency, a figurative hugging of one's own goodness: friendship! at the best, a mere enjoyment of congenial fellowship; at the worst, a prophetic eye to future aggrandisement: filial love! maternal love!—the holiest and best of loves, because in the demonstration there may be, and often is, much to lose and nothing to gain—a homage to self, a falling down before the multiplying Ego, an exhibited admiration for one's second self, one's own reflection in Nature's mirror. Yet every one of these negative virtues may contain some element of unselfishness; but grief, grief for the dead, is solely, wholly and absolutely selfish, unless it arise from a belief that the departed soul is gone to endless punishment; and in this belief, thank God, very few of us remain to-day. No philosopher, no sage of ancient nor modern time, has ever taught with more terseness, more point, more unanswerable logic, the folly, the impiety, the fault against the dead, the fault to nature, the violation of reason, the gross selfishness in mourning for the dead, than Shakspere has.

To mourn for the dead proves in the mourner one of two things: a complete and absolute selfishness, for he mourns what he has lost, not what the dead has gained, over which, did he truly love, he should rejoice; or he shuts out heaven from his creed, admits either annihilation or eternal punishment, thus desiring to retain for himself what God condemns to nothingness, or clinging to what God hates. To mourn for the dead, therefore, is either to exhibit unusual selfishness or unworthy infidelity. There is no escape; they are rotten apples both, and we *must* choose. We mourn because of our loss, or we mourn because of theirs—which is it? If for our own sake, we must admit the selfishness; if we believe that our beloved dead are in heaven, and yet mourn, we must be envious. Do we grieve over our friend's promotion, our brother's advancement, our mother's, our child's happiness? There is no need to pause for a reply; our common nature gave it years ago—we do not. Then why mourn because our friend, our brother, sister, child or mother, has attained a blessedness which we hope, through the same portals of death, to achieve? Either because there is a flaw in our belief, or there is no margin to the full page of our selfishness. We should rejoice, were we unselfish, wise and consistent, at the death of any one we loved; both for ourselves and for others we should look upon "the stroke of death but as a lover's pinch, which hurts, and is desired." We should welcome it for ourselves, "encounter darkness as a bride, and hug it in our arms," and rather than stay "mortality's strong hand," when stretched out to take from us our beloved, we should exclaim with Kent, in *King Lear*, "Oh, let him pass! he hates him much that would upon the rack of this tough world stretch him out longer."

This is the philosophy that Shakspere teaches or would teach us; the master cannot be blamed if we, the pupils, are dense and unapt to learn. In three of his most serious plays—namely, in *Hamlet, King Lear,* and *Romeo and Juliet,*—does he point out, in a way there is no mistaking, the folly, the impiety and the selfishness of mourning for the dead. In the two plays first-named, he deals with the folly and the impiety; in the last, he deals with the selfishness, and with an argument the logic of which defies all refuting powers; and this time he makes a most holy and learned friar his mouthpiece. The parents mourn the death of their child, and it is thus the man of God admonishes them :—

> " Heaven and yourself
> Had part in this fair maid; now Heaven hath all,
> And all the better is it for the maid:
> Your part in her you could not keep from death;
> But Heaven keeps his part in eternal life.

. . . .

> The most you sought was—her promotion ;
> For 'twas your heaven she should be advanced;
> And weep ye now, seeing she is advanced,
> Above the clouds, as high as Heaven itself?"

. . . . . .

All the sophistry in the world—and the world is large and full of it—cannot lessen the truth and wisdom that Shakspere would inculcate. There are few things in life to be desired; every reason why death should be welcome. Is there any one living of whom it may not well be said, " Nothing in this life became him like the leaving of it"—I do not mean in a harsh and cruel sense, but in the sense that we *become* better by the translation ?

Essay II.

PLAYS AND PLAYWRIGHTS.

"The purpose of playing, whose end, both at the first and now, was and is, to hold, as 'twere, the mirror up to Nature; to show virtue her own feature, scorn her own image, and the very age and body of the time his form and pressure."
Hamlet, Act iii. sc. 2.

"I have heard
That guilty creatures, sitting at a play,
Have, by the very cunning of the scene,
Been struck so to the soul, that presently
They have proclaimed their malefactions."
Hamlet, Act ii. sc. 2.

ALTHOUGH Hamlet spoke the words beginning "The purpose of playing" to an actor, and was directly speaking of acting, it is understood that Shakspere refers to the Drama as being a mirror that is held up to Nature. The whole of the first passage above quoted applies more to the dramatist than to the actor. There are few lessons, whether as to goodness, morals or wisdom, that Shakspere taught that he did not illustrate in his own conduct. He was no sign-post that could only point the way: he was a guide who led. To teach by precept is no such difficult matter; your easy-chair pilots have ever existed in swarms since an inhabited world began. He was an active pilot, who took the helm and steered his vessel into port.

"To hold the mirror up to Nature, show virtue her own feature, scorn her own image, and the very age and body of the time his form and pressure,"—this is the work of the play-wright, if he know and love his art. What he represents on the mimic stage must be a reflection of the world—the great stage on which we all strut, play our parts, well or ill, then make our final exit. He must not only show us what the world is like, but in what it is most unlike the thing it should be. There must be no false coloring for the sake of effect, no drawing an improbable condition of things from his own inner consciousness for the sake of harmony; no reflection, in short, from a blotched or ill-shaped glass. The mirror may be small when the dramatic instinct is not great, but it must be true. The virtue he would have us love must be clothed in spotless white; her features must be clearly seen, her beauty must be transcendent, her form of matchless shape, so that the most vicious and criminal of his audience shall inwardly bow the knee and pay her rightful homage.. Around the vice or sin he would depict there must be no false halo of superficial goodness, no show of greatness of soul to hide a want of principle; the moral odiousness must be lettered in capitals, so that the groundlings may have no need of spectacles. Lastly, he must depict the age in which he lives; he must regard himself as the historian of society, to whom future ages will look for a faithful picture of his time.

This is the real work of the dramatist, and this is what Shakspere did. He upheld a mirror that could not lie, that reflected not only the positive, the practical, the average form of things, but their differences, their distinctions; all the lights and shades were true; never too bright, never too dark. He used his fancy, his poetic imagination, to embellish the real, not to create the ideal. He won our love of virtue by no stagey hyperboles, no clap-trap of over-wrought pathos, but by producing her in all her native moral beauty, that captivates the remnant of the divine within us. He never makes us laugh at virtue, even in our sleeves, nor laugh aloud with vice; and if at times we cannot repress an inward chuckle, we rejoice because it is hidden. He made all good things lovable by the very strength of their goodness; he made crime and sin hideous and hateful, vice and folly contemptible and ridiculous.

This, I say again, is the only real and

praiseworthy work that the play-wright has before him; and I say it the more emphatically, because this high and noble branch of literature has degenerated, because our modern dramatists, for the most part, think that the highest ambition of their art is attained when they can make us laugh, and, in lieu of imparting wholesome instruction, which would bear to-morrow's reflection, send us away with a mere sense of having been amused for an hour.

Modern drama,—more especially that branch of it termed Comedy, which Dryden very aptly describes as a representation of the lighter faults of mankind,—has sunk, with but few exceptions, into broad-grinning farce; for farce it is, however deftly our playwrights, or their apologists, may try to disguise the fact by misapplied terms. You may call a man by a false name, and strangers be deceived, but his friends will know him by the right one. There is all the difference in the world between the merry sound of the laughter that is provoked by a delicate touch in true comedy, and the hilarious and noisy convulsions of merriment called forth by a rape on the English language in the shape of a rude pun, or by rough horse-play in an impossible scene. The general light-headedness and frivolity of the age have led our dramatists to pander to depraved tastes—not, I honestly believe, merely to gain the plaudits of unworthy hands, but for bread's sake; the stomach must look to the wit when it cannot look to the hands, and the wit must please the paymaster.

This, it is readily granted, may be the case with some, but with many it is not; they have made their "pile," the growl of the wolf is never likely to be heard again, their names are sufficiently well known to the public to carry weight, and managers will not refuse their wares. It is to such men we have a right to look for high-class work, good enduring literature, that shall raise the English stage to a platform for the teaching of noble aims, of sound, wholesome, and manly doctrine; make our theatres temples for the higher education of the people. Properly utilised, the stage might supplant the pulpit as a teacher; for, whilst the latter can, at the best, but theorise, the former can illustrate and demonstrate the moral it is sought to inculcate. I do not deny that the dramatist who can make us laugh, and so forget for the time-being our petty griefs or deeper sorrows, is a benefactor to his kind in a world so full of cares as ours; but he who can also make us reflect, and thereby make us better, is not only a benefactor in this sense, but a pioneer in the great cause of progressive civilization.

To-day there seems to be no aim to do good, no motive but the unworthy one to cause mere laughter. Schlegel* points out, that whilst Shakspere always had some high moral aim in his plays, he did not neglect the comic element, but like a true artist made it subservient only, not the main feature. He says: "Shakspere's comic talent is equally wonder-

---

* *Lectures on the Drama,* ii. 145.

ful with that which he has shown in the pathetic and tragic; it stands on an equal elevation, and possesses equal extent and profundity. All that I before wished was, not to admit that the former *preponderated.* He is highly inventive in comic situations and motives. It will be hardly possible to show whence he had taken any of them; whereas, in the serious parts of his drama, he has generally laid hold of something already known. His comic characters are equally true, various, and profound with his serious. So little is he disposed to caricature, that we may rather say many of his traits are almost too nice and delicate for the stage; that they can only be properly seized by a great actor, and fully understood by a very acute audience. Not only has he delineated many kinds of folly; he has also contrived to exhibit mere stupidity in a most diverting and entertaining manner."

Thus, even in his comic characters, Shakspere would impart something, if only a higher and subtler sense of humour. But to teach us, make us better, stood first with him. Who can read or witness *Othello*, and not feel how unworthy a passion is jealousy, how unmanly, how insane is anger; how more than foolish it is to believe a knave to the undoing of our own happiness? or *Hamlet*, and not learn how horrible, how soul-blasting is the crime of murder, how base and degrading is unnatural lust? or *Lear*, and not understand how inordinate vanity is akin to madness, and incites a man to commit the actions of an idiot; and how vile a thing is filial ingratitude, a crime that shall carry its own punishment? or to any of the great poet's works, and not learn something worth the learning? and then tell me to what theatre I can go to-day for anything, but to see a tear or two dropped, and hear a half-suppressed snivel over the imaginary woes of an impossible person, or to join in the laughter created by the "clown" in a farcical comedy, who has gone in for the "pitiful ambition" of speaking more than was set down for him?

I have purposely avoided making any comparisons between our living writers; but having said that our modern plays for the most part teach nothing, I am bound in justice to name an exception—Tom Taylor's "Ticket-of-Leave Man." This excellent drama, to my own knowledge, has done much good; in the hearts of many, it has "tempered justice with mercy;" it has proven that a man may not be wholly bad because he has fallen from the pinnacle of divine and human law. It has done more: it has turned the sinner and made him repent, touched his better nature; and if he has not "proclaimed his malefaction," he has at least made reparation, and, we may hope, "sinned no more." This, I again repeat, is the aim of the Drama, and this, I positively assert, has been lost sight of in the present day.

It is to our writers, our authors, in whatever capacity, that the world looks, and has a right to look, for guidance and direction; the power to teach and direct is the highest gift that the Divine mind has seen fit to bestow on man; and woe betide the mortal so endowed who hides or perverts his talent, or seeks to barter it for "the yellow slave" alone!

Essay III.

FAME.

"Spirit, with divine ambition puff'd,
Makes mouths at the invisible event,
Exposing what is mortal, and unsure,
To all that fortune, death, and danger dare—"
Hamlet, Act iv. sc. 4.

"'Tis but a base, ignoble mind
That mounts no higher than a bird can soar."
Henry VI., Part ii. Act ii. sc. 1.

AMONG the almost countless blessings— I can employ no meaner word—for which the world is bound in lasting gratitude to its greatest genius, I know of none that calls for deeper thankfulness than the encouragement, both by example and by precept, given to aspirants for fame by their gentle yet all-powerful master. And yet the little world at Stratford, in which Shakspere moved and had his being, would have made him a lawyer. The notion is so grim an irony, that I must perforce dwell upon it for a short time. This literary giant, this mental Hercules, the man who has " grasped all the diversities of rank, sex, and age—who portrayed the king, the courtier, the courtezan, the hero, the pickpocket, the savant and the fool, and all with equal truth,"—who gave us not imitations, but gave us an insight into Nature as she is,— whose women, unlike the women of other writers, were not copies one of the other, but each having an individuality, an identity of her own, as in life itself,—the only man who actually mastered the greatest of all problems —female character;—this unbound Prometheus, who, by the fire of his genius, can transport us to distant ages and foreign climes, who can one moment embue us with the spirit of the ancient Roman, and the next transform us, as actors, into French fops ; who takes us into the cultivated society of his time in one play, and in another translates us into the barbarities of the past ; the magician, who can call up impossible monsters, like Caliban the dwarf, and Aaron the Moor; exhibit to the inward eye " witches and their unhallowed mysteries;" create fairies, pigmies, and sylphs, so truly, so accurately, that the superstitious believe in their existence, and the sceptic is led to doubt his own reasoning; this intellectual angel in a world of semi-devils, the pride of the civilized universe, the boast of this little island—William Shakspere —they would fain have made a lawyer. *They*, his world (and its counterpart exists to-day), would, had they power, chain the lark to the soil, or, at least, freight his wings in his heavenward flight, cage the eagle in a doll's mansion, rear a hothouse for the giant oak. Shakspere, the light of dramatic literature, the first planet in the starry firmament of poetry, the man who flashed upon this dull world and astonished its inhabitants like the first daring gleam of lightning, *they* would have bound to earth, and made him one of its common worms!

In canty phraseology, we are told that

"we are all worms;" but a dramatic lion has added that "we don't all glow." We all desire to glow. The ignoble mind is satisfied to shine with gold; but Shakspere, whom even the money-worms reverence and worship, even when they understand him not, laboured that he might shine with the luminous glory of intellect. He possessed the desire, "the divine ambition," to raise himself above "the barbarous multitude," to show his Creator that in him the image of the Godhead was no blurred negative, that his claim to a mansion in the kingdom of many was a just one; for intellect is as much an attribute of the All Wise as any virtue within the grasp of meaner capacities.

He felt that "ignorance is the only curse of God, knowledge the wings wherewith we fly to heaven;" that even as man shall elevate his soul here by knowledge, and elevate others through that knowledge, so shall he elevate his status and theirs in the world to come. Let none question the "pass" of the righteous man; but neither let it be questioned that intellect that has raised the possessor, that has raised others, that has worked aright for the bettering of man, shall occupy a place in Paradise.

Shakspere was not content to live and work alone for his own glory; he taught literary aspirants, by noblest precepts and by heroic example, how to labour and to wait, so that now they are content to lie at his feet, and look with upturned eyes into his godlike face for inspiration. It is he who has taught them more than any other man to look beyond "this sterile promontory, the earth," who has infused them with the supernatural glow of "divine ambition." By one all-powerful touch of his all-powerful pen, he has made more authors—men who lead the herd from earth to Paradise—than every touch by other men essayed; than any combination of felicitous accident that has launched some writers on the uncertain sea of authorship.

When the young genius or youth of talent turns his mind to literature, he will find no sympathiser, none who will encourage him like Shakspere; kith and kin will be against him, his best friends will blow hot and cold, as they think he may succeed or fail; his mere acquaintance will ridicule the notion of his possessing the requisite ability;

D

his well-wishers will be too timid to give him a word of hope; his literary circle, if he have one, will endeavour to dissuade him, for each one in that circle thinks himself a god, and that thou shouldst have no other god but he; for he is a jealous god. All the world—his world—will raise its palm against him; and worst of all, there will be times when he himself will be his strongest foe; when he has borne within him, engendered by the opposition on all sides, the brow of painful reflection; when he seems to see his sun of hope dimmed by the envious vapours of night; when, in his self-sought solitude, he feels his mind sink within him, and a "profound sadness cling to his heart like a malady;" when his young desires seem blighted by an untimely frost, and his youth staggered by "the strange apparition of unfriendly ghosts;" when his powers of action are, for the time, sapped up by thought, and his utter bitterness of soul renders him careless of consequences—then let him turn to Shakspere, and in these lines find new incentive to work, fresh motive for raising himself above the "beasts" of his world: "What is a man, if his chief good and market of his time be but to sleep and feed? —a beast, no more?" Truly, it is essential that the literary aspirant should feel, should know, that he has the necessary power within him; for woe betide the luckless wight who fails through his own weakness; not only must he know how to steer his sea-tossed vessel in time of danger, but he must know how to swim in time of wreck. To no weakling, to no mental pigmy, "seeking the ambition that shall overwhelm him," can the bay-leaves of victory be awarded: such will only be sea-sick e'er the anchor is weighed. It is only to the morally brave, to the strong in self-conscious power, to whom the great pilot speaks; but when such a one is doubtful of his own ability, and modesty can make the greatest hero blush; when he feels driven to the wall by the fear of evil result, rather than attracted by the prospect of good; when his mind is so depressed by the snorting of pearl-despising swine, and "he anticipates censure, and is without hope of praise;" when "he dreads a miscarriage, and imagines his diligence will be without reward;" when, indeed, he oscillates, like a tide, between going out as a wave that shall be lost in the ocean of commonplace, or coming in like a stream that shall supply the thirst of those who are far from the shore;—let him once more look to Shakspere and take courage. "Sure He that made us with such large discourse, looking before and after, gave us not that capability and god-like reason to rust* in us unus'd."

---

* In some editions this word is printed "fust." The meaning, however, is much the same.

Essay IV.

SUPERSTITION.

"We defy augury; there is a special providence in the fall of a sparrow. If it be now, 'tis not to come; if it be not to come, it will be now; if it be not now, yet it will come."
Hamlet, Act v. sc. 2.

"Look, how the world's poor people are amaz'd
At apparitions, signs, and prodigies,
Whereon with fearful eyes they long have gaz'd,
Infusing them with dreadful prophecies:"
Venus and Adonis.

"No natural exhalation in the sky,
No scope of Nature, no distempered day,
No common wind, no customed event,
But they will pluck away his natural cause,
And call them meteors, prodigies, and signs,
Abortives, presages, and tongues of Heaven."
King John, Act iii. sc. 4.

CONTEMPT for others or for the failings of others is seldom felt, or, if felt, still less seldom exhibited, by men endowed with great minds or large understandings. Shakspere never, in all his multitudinous writings, has penned a line that could be construed into conveying that he entertained a feeling of contempt for any fellow creature, or for the weakness, vice, or failing of one. For crime and sin he shows a strong and manly hatred; for the criminal his condemnation has a leaven of mercy, and his censure of the sinner is ever softened by pity. But for the weaknesses, failings, and even vices that are the out-growth of mere ignorance, he exhibits the tender, gentle pity that the learned feel for the untaught, the teacher for the pupil. A genius like Shakspere is of no nationality, of no class and of no race. Genius cannot be localised ; it belongs to and is of the world. Hence Shakspere is devoid of bigotry, and is absolutely without prejudice of any kind. He speaks of all nations, of all creeds, of all classes, as though he sat in the clouds—a spectator and historian of the world. Genius is essentially cosmopolitan. Though bound physically in a nut-shell, it counts itself mentally a king of infinite space. Without bigotry, without prejudice, without superstition himself, and yet without contempt for any one whose undeveloped, untaught or uninspired mind might cherish any one of these, or all three. Without bigotry, because he could grasp the good in all religion ; without prejudice, because of no nationality ; no class, because, though born of the people, he was an aristocrat in feeling, in taste, and in love of refinement; without superstition, because, and simply because, no large mind, no specially God-created soul like his could harbour so mean, so poor, so evil a thing as superstition. The very beasts are free from it, because they are liberated from that great blessing, but sometimes equally great curse—imagination. Imagination! a ship that sails safe to harbour with a navigating captain, a vessel that goes to destruction in the first storm with a mutinous crew. Prejudice and superstition are the primary indications of weak minds. Prejudice indicates the untravelled, the unexpanded mind. Superstition denotes the mind upon which nursery tradition has taken a permanent hold. Nothing too silly, nothing too absurd, but such a mind enrolls in its credulous faith.

It is painful and pitiful to see, even in this fairly enlightened age, men and women, whose education one would hope would be the means of plucking out the viler weeds of vulgar superstition, still clinging with unworthy tenacity to " beliefs" born of gross ignorance among the very poorest and most unenlightened of the lower orders. Such " belief," for instance, as the ill-luck attending a journey or an important undertaking on a Friday; the ill-luck consequent upon passing under a ladder, of upsetting the salt, of crossing knives, of seeing the new moon for the first time through glass, of thirteen sitting at table, the crowing of a cock before daybreak, breaking a looking-glass, certain dreams too numerous to mention, and so on, down to the very lowest depths of puerile inanity—these, and such as these, claim a place in the minds of many persons who have received what is termed a liberal education ; and, I regret to add, in the minds of those who, from the position they occupy as writers, should be educators of the people. A writer in . . . . . recently gave his readers five columns anent the remarkable prophecies of the Brahan Seer (Cimneach Odhar Fiosaiche.) He tells us, in all seriousness, that this ignorant, uneducated person possessed a piece of crystal into which he looked and saw the future of any person named. We are informed that, according to tradition (the writer omits to add that *tradition* is often another word for lie), this Brahan Seer once pronounced a prophecy concerning the family of Macleod. Here it is, as given by the author of the book. I quote from notes and memory.

There had been a traditionary prophecy, couched in Gaelic verse, regarding the family of Macleod, which received a most extraordinary fulfilment. It was prophesied at least a hundred years prior to the fulfilment. Here is the wonderful prophecy. It was foretold by this Seer, so says tradition, that when Norman, the third Norman, the son of the hard-loved English lady, would perish by accident—that when the rocks on the well-known coast of Macleod's country became the property of a Campbell,—when a fox had young ones in one of the turrets of the castle, and especially when the fairy enchanted banner should be for the last time exhibited,—then the glory of the Macleod family should depart, &c., &c.

"Now," as the author of the book says, "for the curious coincidence of its fulfilment." It appears that in the castle of the Macleods there was a chest, and this chest was forced open, and in it was the fairy flag. (I suppose it would be too curious to inquire where the fairies got the paper of which the rag was made, that made the flag.) This flag, we are told, had crosses wrought in gold threads, and several elf-spots stitched in silk with great care on different parts of it. When this remarkable chest was opened, the news of the death of the young heir of Macleod reached the castle. Norman, the third Norman, met his death in the *Queen Charlotte*, which was blown up at sea. At the same time the rocks before alluded to were sold to Angus Campbell, of Ensay, and a fox in the west turret of the castle had young ones. "Thus," says the author, "all that was said in the prophecy was fulfilled, although I am glad to say the family still enjoy their ancestral possessions, and the worst part of the prophecy remains unverified."

A rare prophet this truly! A half-demented, half-knavish, low-born, uneducated Scotchman, with a bit of glass, imposes upon the credulous of his time, and upon those who to-day receive the garbled tradition as though it were Holy Writ; and the author who brings before our notice to-day the so-called prophecies of this misnamed Seer, in all seriousness asks his readers to believe. He is glad, he says, that the worst part of the prophecy remains unverified ; and it would appear that the period for its possible verification has lapsed ; yet does he still believe in the *Seer*. What a prophet! and oh, what a disciple!

There are, perhaps, few things easier than the trick of making appear like prophecies the words and writings of those who spoke or wrote much many years ago,—the trick of construing words into meaning what the construer desires, but far from the meaning of the original speaker or writer.

The gift of being able to look into the future is a great and fearful one ; a gift that the Creator would only give to certain men for certain and defined beneficent reasons. It is an insult to common sense, and, far

worse, an insult to our common faith in a
Providence, to entertain for one moment the
belief that this precious and holy gift is ever
bestowed upon such poor and worthless
imitations of fair humanity as the Brahan
Seer and Mother Shipton, who make use of
their pretended powers for the worst of
purposes—the robbing of "credulous fools,"
who "are as tenderly led by the noses as
asses are"—the gratification of petty spite
and malice, the disguising of common ignorance and knavery under the cloak of an
uncommon wisdom and goodness. There
are many otherwise good and worthy persons in our own day, who profess a belief
in the prophecies of Mother Shipton, and
who even now are wearing out their
knee-caps in anticipation of "the crack

of doom" in eighteen hundred and eighty-one.

Mother Shipton wrote her so called prophecies in crude, childish rhyme; and having written the line, "And the end of the world will come," the old woman's brain laboured for a suitable word wherewith to rhyme, and was finally delivered of the word "one," as the nearest numerical approach.

The worthy persons who believe in this old idiot, one ward removed, are highly offended if you point out to them that their belief in this hag is not consistent with their profession of faith in Providence, and they come down upon you as though they would becudgel your brains with words; for these worthies, being weak in logic, are often strong, after a sense, in words. They attend, as my text-giver elsewhere observes, "a feast of the languages, and come away with the scraps."

A true, consistent faith in Providence must of necessity "defy augury." The rulings of the Divine Judge cannot be influenced by the mere accidents that must ever attend poor humanity. Shakspere's faith in Providence was as absolute as his scepticism in aught that savoured of superstition. His logical mind grasped at once the fact that the lesser could not contain the greater. Once given a Providence, and it became impossible that human good or evil could be influenced by human accident. He distinguished with great clearness the difference between the laws of nature, and the mere coincidences, accidents and phenomena that puzzle the unthinking.

It may be thought by some that because Shakspere, ever true to nature, makes many of his characters give vent to some of the superstitions of his day, that he endorses belief in them. A comparison of all that Shakspere has said on a subject will lead the student to distinguish between the sentiments he held, and those he thought fit, for dramatic purposes, to put into the mouths of his characters.

For instance, no one would assert that Shakspere shared in Cæsar's superstition respecting lean men; yet how plausible are the words he gives Cæsar to explain his reasons for disliking thin men, and liking "fat, sleek-headed men."

It has often been urged in argument anent superstition, that no poetic or imaginative mind can be wholly free from it, and that scepticism in small, harmless beliefs such as I have mentioned, denote the hard-headed, practical, mathematical, matter-of-fact individual, who has no poetic sympathies in his nature. This sounds very well, and as if it were true, or at least ought to be true. But facts are opposed to its being true. There have been, and are, many men, poets, dramatists, and singers of divine prose, without an atom of faith in vulgar superstition, and prominent among them is the sceptic Shakspere.

Essay V.

EDUCATION.

> Ignorance is the curse of God.
> *Henry VI.*, Pt. ii. Act iv. sc. 7.

> I held it ever,
> Virtue and cunning were endowments greater
> Than nobleness and riches ; careless heirs
> May the two latter darken and expend ;
> But immortality attends the former,
> Making a man a god.
> *Pericles*, Act iii. sc. 2.

THERE is no theme of permanent interest among men and women of to-day more weighty than that of the education of the masses. The fact has dawned at last like a tardy sun on the leading spirits of the age, that the cause of all earthly unhappiness, of all vice and crime, is the want of that knowledge which is light, for "there is no darkness but ignorance." Dispel that monster altogether, and we have perfect and permanent light; dispel it but a little even, and by that little shall there be more light. In the great prison-house of earthly life, there lies within the compass of every man and woman the power, the means to let in upon their fellows more light; and every portion, every particle removed from the great walls prejudice, bigotry, superstition, helps to let in upon our prison-house one more ray of the divine sun—knowledge.

Many and varied are the objections raised by some people to educating the masses.

Let us for a moment take some of their most plausible objections; for they can be plausible, and even thereby may convert some to their side, since plausibility works upon the ignorant and unthinking as does logic on the wise and thoughtful. They say, then, that by giving the lower orders more knowledge, we shall endanger good order and the preservation of proper social distinctions; that such improvement would only tend to elate them to an undue and even extravagant estimate of themselves. That they would sit in judgment on their betters, that more rights or pretended rights would be born of their vanity, and in fine, that since an augmentation of mental development can be used for bad as well as good purposes, the result of educating the lower orders would but create fresh evil and misery. The answer is simple and easy. The objectors, without knowing it perhaps, draw a line to the knowledge that it is desired should be imparted, and thus leave the pupils not much better off than they were before; one eye opened with a cast in it, and the other permanently blind.

There is no limit to the knowledge that is desired by those who advocate the education of the masses, and the evils which the objectors fear, could only arise, if they arose at all, from imperfect knowledge. Even admitting, under protest, that during the progress of education fresh evils arose, still as each succeeding generation, by natural advancement, and new discoveries in every branch of art, science and philosophy, would be wiser and better than the preceding, the newly created evils would vanish one by one to give place to newly created virtues.

In effect, say the objectors, the goal of complete or almost complete knowledge is far off, and no man and no generation of men can in his or its life attain that goal; the road is thousands of miles in length, and you die ere you have travelled them. This is the plausible net cast in the ocean by those who want things to rest as they are; and many are the minnows,—and let us be thankful they are but minnows,—who are caught. Their argument betrays that old skeleton of egotism—"After me, the deluge;" when I am dead the world has no existence. Why, they ask, should we travel ten miles on that hilly, troublesome road, and then die there? And the answer?—I fear it never comes to them in this world—Because the next generation will have ten miles less to travel.

One of the characteristics of the objector's mind is its muddy denseness. You can reduce a mental fortification of stone or iron, by logical hard hitting, but your argumentative cannon-balls only get buried and lost in a muddy fortification. You, the advocate, start an argument with your adversary, the objector, and the result will be something after the following :—

Advocate—The duty of a human being has many branches; connected with all of them are various general and special considerations to induce and regulate the performance. It must be well, then, that these duties be defined with all possible clearness.

Objector—Yes; but it is better for the great majority of men to be kept in ignorance of the duties you would define. Being ignorant, you may force them to fulfil these duties without understanding them, with understanding, they might question the expediency.

(Mark the *logic* of the objector—*understanding*, yet losing sight of the expediency—where is the understanding?)

Advocate—Will you admit that the rule, or set of rules, by which the conduct of the lower orders toward those above them is to be directed should appear to them *reasonable* as well as being distinctly defined?

Objector—The rule, or set of rules, is

good; but if in ignorance he obeys, I do not see the wisdom of making him understand the reason of his obedience.

Advocate—Surely you will admit it is a nobler thing to have a competent understanding of all that belongs to human interest and duty?

Objector—So long as the duty is performed, it cannot matter whether the performance comes by coercion, instinct, or understanding. You make your dog obey you, but you are at no pains to make him understand why he should.

Here the Advocate, if he have any self-respect, gives over; for he feels he has been playing a game of biggest fool wins, and that he is completely beaten. He also feels that education has done very little for the objector, and that this is consequently a real argument against education. But his own education, it is to be hoped, has brought some philosophy with it. He remembers what is the average number of fools to one wise man, and he is further consoled by the knowledge that the fools help to support the wise, and he is not without hope that the time will come when the wise shall keep the few fools in their proper place—asylums.

The objectors to the education of the lower orders have created a new set of commandments: the first is, "Thou shalt not go into the water till thou hast learnt to swim;" and the second is, "Since thou canst not eat a loaf at a sitting, thou shalt not have a slice."

This in all honesty is the substance of

their argument. They cannot or will not see that all education is a question of gradation. That their own children should commence at A, B, C, and end by taking honours at the University, is a natural course of events ; but that a nation, or a class in the nation, should go through the same course, from the simple to the difficult, from the little to the greater, never enters their minds. The objectors, as a rule, have a great objection to a simile or analogy unless it tend to prove their theory ; hence they treat a nation in its infancy being compared to a child as absurd.

The objectors, again, are usually sycophants, and have a blind admiration of Shakspere. I say a blind admiration : they see neither his merits nor his faults, but they hear of his greatness through the voice of authority, and they are willing to accept the greatness for granted, and admit cheerfully that, as a rule, his words are the words of wisdom; but without a guide they are apt to quote Shakspere as the Devil is said to quote Scripture—"for his purpose:" they ignore the context. Thus, taking the line, "Ignorance is the curse of God," their piety is immediately aroused; and casting up their eyes, they exclaim, "Ah, exactly; we must submit with Christian fortitude to God's curse." They are so ready and so quick in this upcasting of the eyes, that the context, in this case the next line, escapes them: "Knowledge, the wing wherewith we fly to heaven."

Knowledge is the blessing, ignorance the

curse; if one submits to the latter, we shall evidently lack the pinion which the former bestows.

These are grand and noble words, worthy of the great man who gave them birth :—

> "I held it ever,
> Virtue and cunning were endowments greater
> Than nobleness and riches."

The word "cunning" is used in the sense of learning; no one will question the superiority of virtue to aught else; but very many, I fear, would prefer either titles or riches to learning.

The old arguments on education, the decrease of poverty, the decrease of vice, are worn threadbare, and in this essay would be out of place. Shakspere, who is my guide and text-giver, takes the highest and noblest view of mental development. He ranks virtue and knowledge as twins, brother and sister :—

"Study
Virtue and that part of philosophy
. . . . that treats of happiness,
By virtue specially to be achieved."

Essay VI.

WOMAN'S OBEDIENCE.

"Why are our bodies soft and weak and smooth,
Unapt to toil and trouble in the world,
But that our soft conditions and our hearts
Should well agree with our external parts?"
Taming of the Shrew, Act v. sc. 2.

"A woman's heart, which ever yet
Affected eminence, wealth, sovereignity."
Henry VIII., Act ii. sc. 3.

IN Shakspere's play of *Taming of the Shrew* there is an evident design and a regular plot, wherein that design is elaborated and in the end completed. No husband whose wife has never so small a taint of the shrew should fail to study, and study carefully, the means by which Petruchio made so absolute a shrew as Katherine into a good, loving and obedient wife.

The germ of all womanly virtues was only dormant in this would-be Xantope, but she was cursed by ungovernable self-will, which could only be got the better of by a stronger will; her perversity was like the perversity of the mule, which could only be conquered by a still greater and even more ridiculous perversity; hence Petruchio assumes the perverseness of a lunatic, but a lunatic in his senses,—a madman with a method. He works a perfect miracle. The woman when he first married her contradicted him in everything, obeyed him in nothing; ere they have been six months married all is changed, —she contradicts him in nothing, and obeys him in everything. When she first married she was cursed with the notion—so prevalent among her sex to-day—that woman was made to govern, command and sway,—that in most things she was equal to man, in many things his superior. Yet this is the woman, the devil in her being exorcised, who utters this divine lesson, that, did our women take to heart, would turn every domestic hell into a very antechamber of the gods—

> "A woman moved is like a fountain troubled,
>
> . . . . . .
>
> And, while it is so, none so dry or thirsty
> Will deign to sip, or touch one drop of it.
> Thy husband is thy lord, thy life, thy keeper,
> Thy heart, thy sovereign; one that cares for thee
> And for thy maintenance; commits his body
> To painful labour, both by sea and land;

> To watch the night in storms, the day in cold,
> Whilst thou liest at home, secure and safe;
> And craves no other tribute at thy hands
> But love, fair looks, and true obedience,—
> Too little payment for so great a debt.
> Such duty as the subject owes the prince,
> Even such a woman oweth to her husband;
> And, when she is froward, peevish, sullen, sour,
> And not obedient to his honest will,
> What is she but a foul contending rebel,
> And graceless traitor to her loving lord?—
> I am ashamed that women are so simple
> To offer war, where they should kneel for peace;
> Or seek for rule, supremacy, and sway,
> When they are bound to serve, love, and obey.
> Why are our bodies soft and weak and smooth,
> Unapt to toil and trouble in the world,
> But that our soft conditions and our hearts
> Should well agree with our external parts?"

Kate's eloquence and sound reasoning—I am half inclined to think that Petruchio wrote the lines for her, and that she learnt them by heart—had the desired effect upon the women to whom she then addressed herself, and doubtless have had a right good influence upon every woman of Shakspere's time, for the women of his time had not seen, nor heard, nor dreamt of such plagues and pests to society as our modern B——s, G——s, W——s, and the like— peevish, fretful, froward old maids, or else discontented wives with sorry nincompoops for husbands; nor were they tainted *en masse*, as they are to-day, with this pitiful rubbish anent woman's rights, and all the puerile and even loathsome stuff with which the subject teems. But to-day our women are inoculated with the poison so inaptly called Woman's Rights, a poison created by them, and nursed and cultivated into greater growth by the henpecked ninnyhammers who accompany them to the platform, or flatter them by listening to the harangues of these strong-minded hermaphrodites, semi-masculine monstrosities, and applaud to the echo the ravings of these old women, who cackle like pullets over a first egg, and with less reason.

The love of eminence and of sovereignty has carried a large number of the weaker vessels, to-day, beyond all bounds. The she-advocate of female suffrage and woman's rights has entirely forgotten her sex and her sex's proper influence; physically and mentally she longs to have more than Nature intended. She longs for eminence, that she may be proud and disdainful; she desires sovereignty, that she may be cruel and tyrannical. Woman never yet had power but it was to her like a loaded gun in the hands of an infant.

I believe the leaders of this modern craze would, as far as their ideas went, have died a natural death, had it not been for the male idiots who have encouraged them, for the most part, I believe, through absolute fear, being composed chiefly of husbands who dare not call their souls their own, zanies who would simper fondly on their better halves, and caper to a looking-glass with the horns on.

And the hypocrisy of these apologies for men, these accidental, nameless scrapings, is nowhere more apparent than in their treatment of women. To see and hear one of the sorry crew address a lady, one would think he was speaking to a goddess under a temporary cloud, and in need of his attention. Here him talk when no ladies are present, —how the goddess is discussed, sneered at, despised; hear his gross talk, and be ashamed of the accident which compels you to call him a fellow-creature. That such a man should have a shrew to wife is only a just punishment; but the pity is that the punishment is not confined to him,—it extends itself abroad, for she infects other women, who would fain be thought possessed of manly power; and when they have stolen man's power, there is he robbed of it, and there are they unable to use it. They enfeeble a man by their arts and devices, and then, Delilah-like, are complacent over the loss which is not their gain. They hinder him from doing worthy work, and then reproach him because he does not do it.

I think that the present evil of woman's rebellion against her lord and master arises in no small measure from the fact that men encourage "a spirit" in a woman. Too often we hear it said by some man that he likes a woman to have a spirit of her own—so runs the cant phrase; but he lies in his conscience, for he knows that this same "spirit of her own" means a will of her own, and no woman should have a will of her own; her will means wilfulness, her "fitness only comes by fits."

A man may like to see this spirit exhibited on the stage,—it creates fun, it gives animation to the scenes; he may like to witness it well enough in his neighbour's house,—it is food for malicious laughter, a spiteful theme for merriment; but if he be a married man, follow him home, how does he like it then? His wife's spirit either takes all spirit out of him, and he sinks into zanyhood, or it makes his temper the temper of a fiend, and he rules with a rod. If he be a single man, and resolved to marry a woman of spirit, follow the poor deluded wretch from the altar, where you saw him smile the smile of anticipated joy, to his home some months after; mark the corner of his mouth now, and say, what tale does it tell?

So long as woman's mind, heart and soul are in just keeping with her external parts, so long will she rule the world of men for good; so long as woman's ambition is the sovereignty of hearts, so long will she command man's homage with dignity to herself, and without loss to him. Her only spirit must be the spirit of love,—her only will the will of the man.

ESSAYS FROM SHAKSPERE. 85

Essay VII.

HOPE.

" The ample proposition that hope makes
In all designs begun on earth below
Fails in the promised largeness."
Troilus and Cressida, Act i. sc. 3.

"Oft expectation fails, and most oft there
Where most it promises; and oft it hits
Where hope is coldest, and despair most fits."
All's Well that Ends Well, Act ii. sc. 1.

WHILST Hazlitt dwells with pardonable enthusiasm on the wondrous talent exhibited by Shakspere in the delineation of character, whether he dealt with the king or the beggar, the hero or the pickpocket, the sage or the idiot, Schlegel, I think, with more reason, dwells with equal enthusiasm on Shakspere's wonderful power in the exhibition of passion. "If," says Schlegel, "Shakspere deserves our admiration for his character, he is equally deserving of it for his exhibition of passion, taking this word in its widest signification, as including every mental condition, every tone, from indifference to familiar mirth, to the wildest rage and despair. He gives us the history of minds; he lays open to us, in a single word, a whole series of preceding conditions." His passions do not at first stand displayed to us in all their heights, as is the case with so many tragic poets, who, in the language of Lessing, are thorough masters of the legal style of love.

He paints, in a most inimitable manner, the gradual progress from the first origin. He gives, as Lessing says, "a living picture of all the most minute and secret artifices by which a feeling steals into our souls, of all the imperceptible advantages which it there gains, of all the stratagems to it, till it becomes the sole tyrant of our desires and our aversions."

There is not a passion, not an emotion, not a mental condition, not a feeling proper to man, whether created by his physical or his mental nature, upon which Shakspere has not touched; hence Hope, which plays so conspicuous a part in every man's life, is dealt with as only Shakspere could deal with it. Faith, Hope, and Charity are the three emotions common to most men; many men are without Faith, most men are without Charity, but none are without Hope. Hope is the most conspicuous element in every man's Faith, for what he hopes he believes. Hope is the incentive to every man's Charity, for he would not be charitable unless he hoped for reward; yet Hope remains in him though he be faithless and uncharitable.

"It is certain," observes Dr Garth, in his able preface to Ovid's *Metamorphosis*, "that the most hopeful natures are doomed to the greatest number of disappointments." Hope is the one recognised delusion that the wisest and most thoughtful of men, in common with the unwise and the unthinking, not only tolerate, but encourage in themselves and others, from infancy to the death-bed. Nor reason, nor facts, nor failures can ever destroy this will-o'-the-wisp of human existence. In our greatest sorrows, in our most terrible trials, when our best beloved is dead, when ruin, absolute, irrevocable ruin stares us in the face, Hope is the only cup of consolation from which we can freely drink : we hope against reason to meet the beloved dead again ; we hope against facts that our ruin may be a bye-path to splendid fortune. Even in our particular sins, when sullen remorse clutches the heart with an iron grip, or heavenly repentance bids us sin no more, there is still a vague, false, shadowy hope hovering in the dark recesses and musty corners of our nature that the result, the effect of our sins, may yet be for the best.

When the unhappy wife of the ill-fated Richard exclaims—

G

"I will despair, and be at enmity
With cozening Hope: he is a flatterer,
A parasite, a keeper-back of death,
Who gently would dissolve the bands of life,
Which false hope lingers in extremity,"

She lies against humanity. It was as impossible to banish Hope from her nature as it was for her by a word to command light to become darkness. And despite her vehement protest, she betrays in her very next sentence what a hold the "flatterer" has upon her, when she cries out to the next comer, her uncle, who brings tidings of affairs, "For heaven's sake, speak comfortable words"—she still desires to be cheated, still longs to nourish the old delusion.

Since, then, it is impossible to live entirely without this parasite, it behoves the wise and thoughtful to see in how far they can regulate their lives, so that they may temper expectation, and in the end reduce it to moderate proportions—contrive that the "largeness" in promise shall not be greater than the probable reality. The great cynics and satirists of the world have been the men who at first gave themselves wholly up to the pernicious influences of the "flatterer." Their hopes were always so great that their labours to bring about the thing desired were *nil*; their mighty expectations took the place of energy and perseverance; they partook to repletion of the unwholesome food, and slept; when they awoke, of course disappointment stared them in the face.

No satirist has been so bitter in his denunciation of everything beneath the sun as Solomon—not even the canker-hearted

Rochefoucauld. Many writers have attributed Solomon's bitterness towards the close of his career to the reaction that sets in after satiety. No doubt this had no small share in swelling to undue proportions the great man's gall. But I think the larger share is to be found in the penalty attached to unreasonable aspirations, to foolish expectation, namely, great disappointment; and a long series of disappointments finally embitters a man's nature for the rest of his days. Solomon's love of knowledge was so profound that he hoped to achieve more than any man who had gone before him, or any man then living. Of course he fails, and in the end comes his outcry against wisdom and knowledge : " For in much wisdom is much grief, and he that increaseth knowledge increaseth sorrow." Prior to his failure, no one had been so loud in praise of wisdom and knowledge as he. In his early lusty youth his anticipations of the joys of love were boundless; in his odes to the passion he condenses all the fire of Ovid, all the sensuousness of Anacreon; and before his manhood is half-spent, before the hand of time has marked him with the signs of decay, he declares woman to be a snare: "And I find more bitter than death the woman; . . . whoso pleaseth God shall escape her." And so with wine, and so at last with everything. He commenced life as hopeful as an exaggerated Micawber; he ends it as an arch-satirist and a misanthrope. In the dawn of life he was as hopeful and credulous as a school-girl; the rising sun dazzled him, and kept his eyes half closed. In the dusk of life he grew as despondent as Timon, and as sceptical as Voltaire; he saw all things through the mist of eventide. I say that the great cynics and satirists have for the most part been the men who hoped much and proportionately realised but little; through their misdirection the hand of fate turns the milk of human kindness the wrong way, and the sweet becomes sour.

The greatness of every disappointment in life is in exact proportion to the ardour of the hope that animated the expectation of pleasure; and it must be remembered that, as Shakspere says: " The ample proposition that hope makes, *in all designs* begun on earth below, fails in the promised largeness;" hence, I repeat, the wise man will so temper his hope "in all designs" that every anticipated joy, every looked-for pleasure, every desired success, can, after all, be only very minor disappointments. The most poignant griefs in man's life are naturally those arising out of his most serious undertakings ; and perhaps no undertaking is more serious, whether to man or woman, than that of marriage, and the consequent cares and duties of the parent. "Hope," says Shakspere, " is a lover's staff." So much greater the pity! If the lover would but reduce that staff to a switch, he would never walk so far. Before marriage it is not uncommon to hear a young, poetic, sentimental man declare of his beloved that she is an angel. Depend upon it, he believes it, and his hopes of happiness are based upon this insane notion. Such a lover, after three months of married life, will begin to hope there are no such angels in heaven; such a lover will have the longest of faces towards the close of the honeymoon. The wisdom of the saying that marriage is a lottery begins to dawn upon him,—he feels quite certain he hasn't drawn "the grand prize," and hope only induces him to believe he has not drawn a blank. If his friends judge of his prize by his face, they would not entertain the same hope. Touching the hopes before marriage, I am sure women are less foolish than men; and they have their reward, for "oft expectation hits where love is coldest." If "love and reason were better acquainted" before marriage, there would be fewer idiots afterwards, " running up and down seeking to hide their baubles. Cross-examine the pessimists of your acquaintance, and you will discover that once upon a time they were optimists; watch closely the optimists in your circle, and you will find them one day rabid pessimists. Once more, then, true wisdom, while never ignoring the necessity of moderate hope, will never allow immoderate expectation to be the ascendant star whereby life's course is steered. Then of such an one it can never be said—

> " He lined himself with hope,
>   Eating the air on promise of supply,
>   Flattering himself in project of a power
>   Much smaller than the smallest of his thoughts;
>   And so, with great imagination
>   Proper to madmen, led his power to death,
>   And, winking, leap'd into destruction."

Essay VIII.

EXPERIENCE.

> "Who ever shunn'd by precedent
> The destined ill she must herself essay?"
> *The Lover's Complaint.*

> "To wilful men
> The injuries that they themselves procure
> Must be their schoolmaster."
> *King Lear*, Act ii. sc. 4.

IT may be boldly asserted that there is not an adult of either sex to whom the above quoted texts do not apply with more or less force. The value of actual experience cannot be over-rated with regard to many undertakings in life, and wherein the precedent of another's experience would serve but ill to afford one the information sought. On the other hand, there are conditions of being of which it is absolutely necessary we should be master, and concerning which we can learn all through the experience of others, and never expend a metaphorical penny in the acquisition.

I will endeavour to define two of the circumstances of life of which reason bids us learn through the fortune or misfortune of those who have essayed and failed, and left us the rich legacy of their experience. When the maiden in *The Lover's Complaint* bewails the falseness of her swain and her own betrayal, knowing, even as she uttered her cries of despair, she but echoed an old cry that the world has heard so often that it has almost grown callous to the betrayed, and will often laugh with the betrayer, feeling, even when first she listened with burning cheek and throbbing heart to the impassioned words breathed so plaintively and musically in her willing ear, that she might have to encounter the same sad fate of so many of her sex, she gives to every woman such a lesson that those who will not profit by it can scarcely lay any claim to sympathy or compassion from those who have. It is at this most painful juncture in the young woman's life that Shakspere puts the pithy question:

> "Whoever shunned by precedent
> The destined ill she must herself essay?"

The word *must* cannot be rendered in the

sense of meaning *fated*, but rather in the sense of implying a wilful resolve to essay, the object, armed with a most feeble hope that the destined ill that fell to others will not be hers. Nor does the query carry with it the supposition that the answer must ever be the hopeless negative, but is put forth in a way that invites the wisdom of those who possess it, urging them to shun the destined ill which the experience of others has made the safe precedent whereby to steer life's course.

I have taken it for granted that my readers are acquainted with the conditions of life of the lover who was false to the maid, and of the maid who was false to herself, namely, that a wide gulf of social position separated them.

It is the poet Young, I think, who, in *Night Thoughts*, gives utterance to the words, "All men deem men mortal but themselves." This overweening vanity, this fool's reliance in one's own impregnability, leads every young woman who is wooed by one much above her to regard her mirror as a gospel that cannot lie. "My beauty," she mutters to herself, "is sufficient to make any man love me. I know my friend Alice was betrayed by such another man as my lover; so was my neighbour Maud; but then they were *very* different. Alice had a pretty doll's face, but no style; and Maud could really boast of nothing but her figure; whilst I—" Then comes a smile of self-sufficiency, another look in the mirror,—the libertine's best friend, his most trustworthy pander,—a toss of the little flighty head, and she sallies forth to encounter again the gay gallant, who is a perfect master of the art of lying in word and deed. She will never see the cunning smile behind the mask he wears, nor hear the demon-chuckle beneath his protestation of devotion and constancy. She looks at his mask, and deems it his truthful face; she listens to his vows, and thinks them but her rightful due. And yet, within her most secret inner consciousness, there is a small, still voice that tells her that this man seeks her for a something that she should not, dare not give, save under one condition. Then comes the maiden blush to her cheek, and she rebels, but false modesty (and a woman has always more or less of both, the real and the false) bids her turn her back upon the very thought, and she obeys, till true modesty falls a victim to the deed; for there comes a time when the voice of true modesty is hushed, and only the voice of the false is heard,—when "strange love, grown bold, thinks true love *acted*, simple modesty," and when to accuse the act in thought is alone immodest.

It is now that the woman dreams and the man becomes practical. To her Nature has opened the flood-gates of life, and she hears in fancy lovely strains of melody, that seem to be a part of, or to emanate from her. Glorious are the castles in the air she builds, now of a mundane, earthly character—he and she living together supremely happy, walking together arm-in-arm through summer lanes, drinking in the sweet evening air, and listening to the birds as they sing of love,—love as unconventional as their own; or sitting cosily together over the warm winter hearth, he or she reading aloud from some congenial book, words and thoughts that animate them with a sympathetic glow, and draw them closer and closer together; and then her thoughts take a pure ethereal form—they are wandering on and on through infinite space, locked in an immortal embrace, in which their souls have commingled and become wholly one, seeing sights no mortal ever saw, listening to far-off music whose sweetness angels alone can hear and live; on, on for ever and for ever, enjoying a spiritual happiness such as the heart of man fails to grasp. Castles in the air! One brick removed from the basement, and the entire fabric comes to the ground.

The practical *roué* thinks differently; he has played his part upon the stage, and now that all is over, the gas turned down, the furniture draped, his own gay trappings removed, he wants to call a cab and go home to his bachelor's rooms, and he goes with a promise to see the dreamer again. But when they next meet it is in some haunt of vice, where he finds her ready to sell for gold what once was only given for love. The dreamer has become practical, and is miserable; the practical dreams a little, but the nightmare wakes him. So much for the woman who might have learnt from other women "the destined ill she must herself essay."

So long as man allows his reason to dictate the actions of his life, to be the beacon whereby to steer, so long will he keep clear of the rocks and shoals that for ever threaten him; but when impulse, heart, emotion, or, in short, passion of any sort, takes the helm, nothing but chance, or good fortune, can save him from wreck, more or less disastrous. When wilfulness, the scion of a passion, sways a man, the only schoolmaster who can ever teach him is experience.

Most single men regard matrimony as a harbour very desirable to be reached; most married men know it for a pool in which they find themselves in quarentine, because most men, despite the experience of the majority of their male acquaintances, will marry at the dictate of passion of some kind, when reason only should be the arbiter between a man and the burden he will have to carry, generally for life. When a man undertakes matrimony, he enters the race of life more or less heavily weighted; if it serve as ballast for the unsteady, well and good; it will keep him on the course, and he may come in at the finish not an outsider; or, to use another simile, prevent the ship from going over in the fresh gale. If, however, as in the large majority of cases, matrimony is to the man mere superfluous weight—either a very millstone that keeps him at the post, so that he never starts at all, or only a handful of shot that will tell on him at the finish—it is a condition with penalties attached, which a man's reason alone can determine whether or no to accept.

Let every single man consult his married acquaintances before he takes the irrevocable step, and be guided by their advice ; and it is a safe prophecy to predict that the number of unhappy, ill-assorted marriages would be reduced at least eighty per cent. Let the single man take the precedent of the married, and he need never encounter the whip of the schoolmaster—personal experience.

But seldom or never will the single man get absolutely pure, unadulterated advice from the married ; large allowance must be made for that peculiar hypocrisy—some call it philosophy—that induces a man to make the best of a bad bargain. Having bought at a great price a useless article, to confess it is to confess one's self a fool, and so the best is made of it—the bad investment is well advertised, and the fool invests, but he does not advertise his folly. The wise man makes capital out of the fool—out of one man's folly groweth another man's wisdom. Let the wise man who is single grow wiser from the folly of the married fools—they are the wilful men whose injuries must be their schoolmasters ; what the schoolmaster—experience—taught them, be thou wise enough to learn without the schoolmaster. Let the young man say with Benedict :

" I do much wonder that one man, seeing how much another man is a fool when he dedicates his behaviours to love, will, after he hath laughed at such shallow follies in others, become the argument of his own scorn by falling in love."

Benedict was wise then, for his reasoning

was deducted from the experience of others; but when he fell in love with Beatrice, he became the argument of his own scorn. His wisdom, as a bachelor, was folly to the fool; his folly, as a Benedict, should save the wise from foolishness.

Essay IX.

TEMPTATION.

"In each grace . . .
There lurks a still and dumb discoursive devil,
That tempts most cunningly."
Troilus and Cressida, Act iv. sc. 4.

"Oftentimes to win us to our harm,
The instruments of darkness tell us truths;
Win us with honest trifles, to betray us
In deepest consequence."
Macbeth, Act i. sc. 3.

"Most dangerous
Is that temptation that doth goad us on
To sin in loving virtue."
Measure for Measure, Act ii. sc. 2.

IN each of the three plays from which I select my texts, temptation is the great motive force that brings about the incidents, and, in short, constitutes the main feature of the plot,—the thread whereby hangs the tale. Beauty was the cause of Cressida's vanity, which led her to seek, with feminine eagerness, for the admiration of the other sex. In the very grace with which she was endowed there lurked a dumb discoursive devil, that finally induces her to betray her lover, Troilus, when his admiration was no longer a novelty. The temptation in the shape of beauty has ever been a most potent weapon for evil in women. The lust for admiration in a woman has its source in a Nemesis-like love of self that can yield no satisfaction, because the being one's self precludes the possession of one's self; hence creeps in the desire to yield possession to another, and with many, as with Cressida, to extend the number of possessors in proportion to the number of those who admire.

In Macbeth we have a fine exemplification of the fall of a great man through the temptation of an over-weening ambition. He is betrayed into his great crime by honest trifles—there is a power of thought in those two words;—he is told truths by the instruments of darkness that he may eventually fall into sin of deepest consequence. Seeing that, according to tradition, the Evil Spirit fell through ambition, there is no margin for wonder that this passion in man, carried to excess, becomes an almost overwhelming temptation to sin in the hands of "the instruments of darkness."

Angelo, I think, is purposely designed by Shakespere to illustrate that any extreme of love for any one virtue, more especially if the severe adherence to that virtue be opposed to the laws of nature, is a rare bait to sin. The human mind is so wonderfully and strangely constituted that, if a man allow his thoughts to rest too long in the contemplation of any particular sin, which he deems worse than another, and especially desires to avoid, he at once creates a morbid curiosity about it, and there steals into his soul an unhealthy craving ; and then by almost imperceptible degrees he loses his moral delicacy about it, and in a short time he discovers himself unable to resist the temptation he has positively created for himself. He knows it is a bait,—he knows that the Devil is at the end of the rod—yet will he nibble, yet will he finally bite. And the secret lies in this thinking. The evil thoughts that flash through the minds of the bulk of men or women, and

"There is no palace wherein foul things do not enter,"

are not sinful, for they are involuntary. It is only when we, as it were, bar the exit against the ugly visitor, and look upon him until the features grow familiar, that we cease to fear, gradually become fascinated, and in the end succumb. It was by this mental process that Angelo commenced his downward descent. Be it remembered that he has condemned Claudio to death for fornication, and Isabella, Claudio's sister, has been to plead for mercy, and Angelo has been feasting his eyes upon her rare beauty. Listen to his sophistry when once more left alone :—

"What's this? What's this? Is this her fault or mine?
The tempter or the tempted, who sins most, ha?
Not she; nor doth she tempt: but it is I,
That, lying by the violet in the sun,
Do as the carrion does, not as the flower,
Corrupt with virtuous season. Can it be,
That modesty may more betray our sense
Than woman's lightness? Having waste ground enough,
Shall we desire to raze the sanctuary,
And pitch our evils there? Oh, fie, fie, fie!
Dost thou desire her foully for those things
That make her good? Oh, let her brother live!
Thieves for their robbery have authority,
When judges steal themselves. What! do I love her,
That I desire to hear her speak again,
And feast upon her eyes? What is't I dream on?
Oh, cunning enemy, that, to catch a saint
With saints doth bait thy hook! Most dangerous

Is that temptation that doth goad us on
To sin in loving virtue. Never could the wanton,
With all her double vigour, art and nature,
Once stir my temper; but this virtuous maid
Subdues me quite."

This is the prelude. His mind is dwelling on the sin that he should have dismissed with the one involuntary thought. When we next meet him he has become like overripe fruit still hanging to the tree, ready to fall at any moment. Listen once more :—

'When I would pray and think, I think and pray
To several subjects; heaven hath my empty words;
Whilst any invention, hearing not my tongue,
Anchors on Isabel. Heaven in my mouth,
As if I did but only chew his name,
And in my heart the strong and swelling evil
Of my conception."

He has reached that phase of mind when the action, or attempted action, must take the place of prolonged thought. Temptation is often only another word for opportunity. The negative virtue of many consists in the non-appearance of fitting opportunity; yet this same opportunity is a fly in especial favour with the great fisher for souls. But the negatively virtuous are often very wary; their great shield is the dread of exposure, but the mocker of sinners tempts the society lovers with a promise to furnish the means of avoiding exposure, and hence comes the trap. The means prosper, but the sinner is haunted. The means consist of deeds which will still less bear exposure, and they breed fast, they multiply. The deeds committed to hide the one are worse than the original for which exposure was dreaded. Then the fiend, when all is ripe, turns and laughs a hideous laugh, tears off the veil, and then are all your evil deeds exposed to every one. More than this: he tells the sinner mockingly that had it not been for the means he took to avoid exposure, exposure would not have happened at all.

Some writer trying to drag himself into notoriety, recently contributed an article to some second-rate journal, in which he endeavoured to show that Shakspere was immoral in his writings. A scurvy beggar may throw mud at a godly prince; the prince has no difficulty in having the mud removed, the beggar never gets rid of the scurvy. Truly, Shakspere was no moralist in the sense that he tried to find out the bad in everything; his aim was to show " there is some soul of goodness in things evil." His was a grand cosmopolitan mind, and could never descend to mere pedantic, narrow, sectarian moralising. He was, as Hazlitt says, no moralist in one sense; in another, he was the greatest of all moralists. "He was a moralist in the sense that Nature is one. He taught what he had learnt from her. He showed the greatest knowledge of humanity with the greatest fellow-feeling for it." Thus, though he shows how Angelo was tempted, he condemns Angelo; yet is his condemnation tempered by mercy,—he condemns the sin, and spares the sinner.

Essay X.

PUBLIC OPINION.

> "I will not choose what many men desire,
> Because I will not jump with common spirits,
> And rank me with the barbarous multitudes."
> *Merchant of Venice*, Act. ii. sc. 9.

> "A plague of opinion! A man may wear it on both
> Sides, like a leather jerkin."
> *Troilus and Cressida*, Act. iii. sc. 3.

THE *Merchant of Venice*, from which my chief text is taken, was founded upon a novel by Geovanni Florentino, who wrote in 1378. Shakspere took the main incidents of this novel, and the romantic circumstances of the casket—choosing from an old translation of the *Gesta Romanorum,*—and out of these materials wrought the most beautiful, most delightful comedy ever penned by man. It is as superior to any of his other comedies —charming, doubtless, as many of them are—as Toby's *Honeymoon* is to Bulwer Lytton's *Lady of Lyons.* I purposely put these last named plays in juxtaposition, because, though the conditions in life of the heroes are reversed, the plot in the main is the same. But to our text. Shakspere had an absolute contempt of public opinion. He seldom refers to " public opinion," whose representative of course is the multitude, without purposely throwing in an opprobrious epithet. With him it was always " The fool multitude that choose by show,"

"The barbarous multitude," "Our slippery people," "This common body," "The rabble, cats," "The blunt monster with uncounted heads," "The distracted multitude," "The vulgar heart," "The common herd," and so on, almost without exception. As he knew most things intuitively, for there lived none who could teach him,—whether it be the circulation of the blood—as witness, "As dear to me as are the *ruddy drops* that *visit my sad heart;*" or the law of gravitation— as, for example, "My love is as the very *centre of the earth, drawing all things to it;*" or that this little world of ours was suspended in mid air, as when he speaks of the spirit "blown with restless violence *round about* the *pendant* world,"—even so he knew intuitively that the sycophantic, craven, white-livered cry of "Vox populi, vox Dei," as rampant in his own day as in ours, meant, when truthfully translated, "The voice of the people is *not* the voice of God." It is not the first time that the spirit of evil has been taken for the spirit of good. When the duke in *Othello* calls upon the Moor to head the army against the Turk, for "Though we have a substitute of much allowed sufficiency, yet opinion, a sovereign mistress of effects, throws a more safer voice on you," he but admits, in the words "a sovereign mistress of effects," the power of public opinion, not the good nor the truth of it; for though opinion be the sovereign mistress or cause of effects, it too often happens that the effects are·bad,—bad because the cause is not good, the sickly child of a diseased parent, the living, scrofulous abortion of the Hydra-headed populace.

Public opinion must of necessity mean the opinion of the majority, and the majority are mongrel; the majority are the unlettered, the uneducated, the illiterate, the intemperate, the unthinking,—in two words, the "barbarous multitude;" and their opinion is what some time-serving idiot who retained a dim remembrance of his school classics terms the "Vox Dei," voice of God! What god? To answer this question we must discover the kind of god a time-serving idiot would be likely to worship.

To admit for one moment the truth of this clap-trap that makes the voice of a people the voice of truth and right and justice, or, in other words, the voice of God, is to accuse the Creator of the greatest possible inconsistency, not to mention other sins of which nations are too often guilty; for "the common herd" may be likened to the pelican,—what it swallows one minute it emits the next, and digests nothing. They cry out for a new law to-day, and petition for its repeal to-morrow. One minute they cry aloud with Brutus that Cæsar's death was just; on the next they weep over his remains with Antony, and shriek for vengeance. They ever sway like reeds before a cross wind.

The great eloquence of one man can madden a people to any act, be it good or evil, and at the very instant the greater eloquence of another man shall stay them. They know no law of reason, but let their tongues wag like a dog's tail on the smallest provocation. They never guage the future, but act blindly on what appears to them to be good for the present. They ever turn a deaf ear to the voice of Experience, but will listen with rapt attention to Folly, if she but come to them in the garb of Wisdom.

So much, then, for the opinion of the multitude—this public opinion that is like a leather jerkin, and can be worn on both sides. Public opinion has done some good, and may do much more; but its evils and its wrongs far outnumber its "things of good repute."

Unfortunately the great mass carries with it men who know better, but have not the courage of their opinion, nor, perhaps, the mental strength and moral bravery to withstand the ugly power of "the blunt monster;" and so, like fresh green leaves on a muddy stream, they sail on in company with the floating excrements cast from out the cesspool of the fools. How few dare think for themselves! How few are hardy enough to admire what the world dislikes, to hate what the world loves, to raise the hand of an Iconoclast, and dash to pieces some of the stuccoed, worthless, miserable idols of "the fool multitude!"

No, even the thousands who know better must needs toady to fashion, play flunkey to the Great Unthinking,—be in the wrong with the many, because they are not brave enough to be in the right with the few. The author dares not write what is true, but only what is palatable and profitable. There stands the mass in front of him who must be pleased, and at its back stand some of the lettered friends of the multitude, whips in hand, ready to let the lash fall if the author, be he never so truthful, fail to fall in with public opinion. Our writers care not to be exponents of the truth, but eke out their brains by slow degrees in stringing together popular views in well-turned and grammatically put sentences. The divine supplies the style of doctrine most in vogue with his congregation, and for which they pay. He dare not refuse, dare not let his individual conscience speak, for his customers would go elsewhere and buy the articles he declined to serve.

And so it is all round, or very nearly so,— a base and servile spirit, clothed in the garb of sycophancy and hypocrisy, ducking the head to the motley fool, and forcing a laugh at the sound of his silly bells. Many a young man starts in life determined to battle against the wrong, and strike only for the right. He has burning impulses after good; he has the strength and courage of the lion; he is resolved to do much and dare all. Truth, and truth only, is the banner under which he will fight, and never surrender save in death. But in time his brain gets bemuddled with the public cant and foolery of his time. At first he only listens; then he heeds; and lastly, expediency says, "Go with the crowd; be wise, 'put money in thy purse.'" And, worst of all, he listens to the muddy-water and sour-milk religious talk of his age,—to the "tight, umbrella

notions" of old women with and without in-
expressible appendages; and, lo! there is a
metamorphosis,—the strong and courageous
lion has become a weak and timid hare. The
truth he resolved to seek now hounds him,
and he runs to seek shelter amid the reeds
that sway before the wind.

Will it be so always? Will this jumping
"with common spirits," so prevalent to-day,
be of long endurance? Or will the rapid
growth of education make the phrase of
"barbarous multitude," so appropriate now,
an almost forgotten expression in the glorious
days to come? I know that the lovers of
expediency (and who is not politic?) will
urge that to pull against the stream is waste
of time, energy and strength, when sailing
with the flowing tide will land us in a safe

and pleasant harbour. They will argue that to stand in opposition to public opinion is as silly as was the experiment of Ctesiphon, who undertook a kicking match with a mule. I cannot gainsay the apparent logic of their objection. There is a worldly wise philosophy in what the expedientists,—if I may be permitted to coin a word for the nonce— would inculcate. If self-respect be of little worth, they are right ; but if self-respect be of more worth than the respect of the unworthy, they are wrong.

The time may come, though it will not be for the present generation to see, when the dynasty of the people will be the only dynasty that is right,—when its voice shall be the voice of an educated mass that, through knowledge, has approximated nearer to the divine. For inherent in all men's hearts there are burning impulses after right and truth,—waking dreams of a higher life and a loftier destiny; and when these inherent impulses shall have developed into nobler actions, and the dreams be realised, then, and then only, to "choose what many men desire" will not be to "jump with common spirits," nor *to* rank *ye* with a barbarous multitude."

Essay II.

MERCY.

"We do pray for mercy;
And that same prayer doth teach us all to render
The deeds of mercy."
    Merchant of Venice, Act iv. sc. 1.

"Wilt thou draw near the nature of the gods?
Draw near them then in being merciful;
Sweet mercy is nobility's true badge."
    Titus Andronicus, Act i. sc. 2.

I BELIEVE there does not exist a single virtue with which humanity is acquainted —the acquaintance, at best, is but a slight one—that Shakspere did not touch upon, and certainly not one on which he expended so many words, such force, such eloquence as on the virtue of Mercy. Without doubt the key-note for his teachings on this subject was struck by the New Testament, but even there we can find no truer, or more forcible, yet touching lines than—

> " The power that I have on you, is to spare you ;
> The malice towards you to forgive you."

Shakspere has invariably employed the word Mercy in the sense of Charity,—the charity that embraces every good, beside which every other virtue, if it exclude charity, is absolutely worthless,—for charity is the very heart of our moral and mental existence. It is sad to think how the appointed teachers of the world have missed the opportunity for good they might have done. Had they for the last eighteen hundred years and more used their energies, their eloquence, their powers of persuasion to inculcate Charity, instead of inciting men to fight for forms of faith, to quarrel over the very natures and degrees of their hopes—to slay, to imprison, to curse every one his brother man who could not see as much or as little as he saw,—the world we live in to-day would not be the hell it surely is.

I say that our teachers have all in their miserable, blind ignorance done more for the spirit of evil than for the spirit of good. There are no thanks due to them that men in the civilized world are beginning at last to get a dim perception of the truth that Charity is all, and that all else is naught. The grand truth is asserting itself in the minds of the educated—the first rays of the sun has been felt, and we wait and pray for the warmth and light of the full noontide.

It is out of such glaring and stupendous evils as the Russo-Turkish war that much good comes; for though it close for ever the eyes of many men in death, it will open the eyes of many more to the true life. Twice within ten years has war been waged in God's name, His name called upon by the nations' representatives, by their so-called *God's anointed;* and even amidst the din and thunder of the battle's roar, the slaying and wounding, the moans and tears, the painful mockery of prayers for the dying and the dead, men have paused to ask themselves— are we Christians ? What are the attributes of the God invoked ?

As with nations so it is with individuals, —the drop from the ocean has the same elements as the ocean itself. In almost every feud between man and man, each invokes *his* God for help, from the low debased drunkard who exclaims in his brutal fury to the woman he, by chance, has vowed to protect—the which he is bound to do with or without the vow—"So help me God, but I'll do for you yet," to the respectable churchgoing Sabbatarian who prays God in general terms to forgive his or her enemies, but omits with a purpose to name the only one he or she has.

I say again that had Charity—which is the only virtue in all religion,—been taught with the same persistence which has been lavished on the questionably good, the petty, the worthless, and the evil, then the comparative ruffian of the day, if such an one existed, would exclaim, "The power that I have on you is to spare you;" and the church-going Sabbatarian to say, "My malice towards you is to forgive you."

This is the spirit that would exist to-day, but for those who have preached continually —nay, *ad nauseam*—on everything but the one thing, and the one thing that admits of no mental nausea in the repetition. In my own life I have never heard one charity sermon that did not terminate in a collection; alms-giving was the only form of Charity of which the preacher seemed to have any cognizance; its greater elements— mercy, forgiveness, kindness, gentleness—are not dwelt upon, but barely alluded to, as loose tackle pertaining to the mainmast—money.

Shakespere says: "'Tis not enough to help the feeble up, but to support him after." The preacher never gets beyond the helping up; money can do that; the *supporting after* demands the real Christian virtue of Charity in its true sense. I use the word Christian, because Christ taught nothing else,—absolutely, positively *nothing* else. He referred casually to various matters, He insisted upon nothing but Charity; His whole life was a doing of mercy. His death was an act of perfect Charity. The only comparatively harsh words he uttered was against uncharity. He loved the sinner better than he loved the saint, because, though God, He represented man, and he taught us to say, "Forgive us *as* we forgive." That word *as* has more meaning, more true significance for us as Christians than any word or any number of words in the language. "We do pray for mercy, and that same prayer doth teach us all to render the deeds of mercy."

Shakspere had not missed the point. You have no right to pray for nor to expect mercy unless you render the deeds of mercy; there is no forgiveness for the unforgiving. Even as you forgive, as you render the deeds of mercy, as you bear Charity, so will you proclaim the image of God within you. God's children must be like the Father, for a bad portraiture will discover to Him that Nature has played him a harlot's trick—the imprint is Satan's.

Our bard tells us that mercy is "nobility's true badge." Had so rapid a thinker had time to reconsider, I think he would have amended the sentence by saying "nobility's *only* true badge," for there is no nobility without it. There is but one key to the gate of Heaven—Charity. See that you have it; if you have it not, never believe that the gate can be broken open. If you possess it, but have allowed the key to get rusty, see to the oiling; for though the hinges of the gate move with ease, the lock is difficult to turn.

Essay III.

PERSEVERANCE.

"Perseverance, dear my lord,
Keeps honour bright: to have done, is to hang
Quite out of fashion, like a rusty mail
In monumental mockery."
   Troilus and Cressida, Act iii. sc. 3.

"Yield not thine neck
To fortune's yoke, but let thy dauntless mind
Still ride in triumph over all mischance."
   Henry VI., Pt. iii. Act iii. sc. 3.

WHEN Achilles would fain rest upon what he had achieved, Ulysses pours into his ears words of truest wisdom—" To have done, is to hang quite out of fashion, like a rusty mail in monumental mockery." The simile is unmatched; the analogy is perfect. So long as life is in us, so long must we continue to *do;* our past, be it never so brilliant, is mere rusty mail, that only mocks the present.

There is no resting on one's oar in the stormy ocean of life; to cease to pull, is to drift into the trough and be overwhelmed by the pitiless waves. There is no rest, only work. "If you give way or hedge aside from the direct forth right, like to an entered tide, they all rush by, and leave you hindmost." This is the lesson Shakspere would teach us—Perseverance is master to genius. Chatterton dies in a garret for lack of energy and courage; Johnson plods on, and triumphs over Chesterfield. The lack of Perseverance is a disease that can make genius grow dim, become like a shooting star in a firmament of fixed constellations—make talent a mere rocket, a momentary flash, a false promise of illumination—then only a stick and· utter darkness.

The lack of Perseverance is a chronic paralysis to genius; a heart-disease without remedy to talent, that thus dies suddenly. There is no half-heartedness in Perseverance. It must be grasped in its entirety, or not at all. No achievement in the past must satisfy the mind embued with this virtue; to have done is nothing, to do is all; for "what others do in the present, though less than yours in the past, must o'ertop yours," for "Time [used in the sense of popularity] is like a fashionable host, that slightly shakes his parting guest by the hand, and with his arms outstretched, as he would fly, grasps in the comer." It is the world all over. It has only the memory of the drunkard,—a recollection that exaggerates the deeds of worm-eaten heroes, and forgets the achievements of those who yesterday moved the world.

This is the wallet of which our bard speaks, " wherein Time puts alms for oblivion, —a great siz'd monster of ingratitude. These scraps are good deeds past, which are devoured as soon as they are made, forgot as soon as done." To have done is nothing, to do is all. In all grades of society, in all professions, in all phases of life, the principle of action should be to do better and better. The greater the difficulties to be surmounted, the greater should be the energy, the more determined the resolve, the more tenacious the perseverance.

Some writer observes, tamely enough, that, "with few exceptions, those who determine to succeed do so." The triteness of the observation must be forgiven for its truth. It is the dogged determination to succeed—the hope that will not be answered but by experience; the passion of the mind for hidden good, that will not be satisfied but by realization. These, and these only, ever find the "strait so narrow, where one but goes abreast," that terminates in success.

But ever remember success is a bad master, whose servants are often pampered until they degenerate into inertness, and sit with folded hands, content to watch the struggling crowd so eager to dethrone them. To have done is nothing. Bask not idly in the bright rays of yesterday's performance, but work steadily in the sombre shade of ever-existing difficulties for the brighter glory of to-morrow.

It is hard to say whether success or failure be the greater foe to Perseverance. Achievement is apt to make a man content, like Achilles, just as failure has a tendency to make him declare, with the ill-fated wife of Richard II.,

> " I will despair, and be at enmity
> With cozening Hope: he is a flatterer,
> A parasite, a keeper-back of death,
> Who gently would dissolve the bands of life,
> Which false hope lingers in extremity."

Under success one feels inclined to rest,

forgetting that the reactionary tide will leave him hindmost; that the living present is greater than the dead past; that "things in motion sooner catch the eye than what not stirs;" that the open-eyed dwarf is of more importance than the sleeping giant, unless Perseverance stir him to better himself, and outdo the past. The world is ever on the alert to bury achievement, and erect a monument to its memory; but Perseverance should know no death that comes not through heaven's messenger, and should scorn the monument it may live to see.

Under failure one is too apt to feel like the shipwrecked mariner, who hails the vessel which he thinks has seen his signals of distress, and then watches her as she sails on out of sight in stately indifference. The glaring light which a transient hope had flung across his path, becomes as a flash of lightning, which, vanishing, leaves the darkness more hideously real, unless Perseverance create in him the necessary hope that preserves life, even till the final vessel shall heave in sight. Persevere even to the very end; achieve success, but *work* in the service of the Master; eschew the arm-chair pension, and the moral vapours born of idleness. To have done is nothing, to do is all. Nothing succeeds like success, says Talleyrand. True, maybe; but nothing succeeds like success in spoiling Perseverance. Persevere to the very end, though every past attempt be failure—a grim and terrible Frankenstein, whose embrace is death. Heed not Fortune's frown; the wrinkles on her brow to-day may be smooth to-morrow; and even though her smile come not now, "let thy dauntless mind still ride in triumph over all mischance."

Essay XIII.

CONSISTENCY.

"I can easier teach twenty what were good to be done, than be one of the twenty to follow mine own teaching."
Merchant of Venice, Act. i. sc. 2.

"Do not, as some ungracious pastors do,
Show me the steep and thorny way to heaven;
Whilst, like a puff'd and reckless libertine,
Himself the primrose path of dalliance treads,
And recks not his own rede."
Hamlet, Act i. sc. 3.

BOTH in the comedy and the tragedy from which the above extracts are taken, Shakspere exemplified the truth which he put into the mouths of Portia and Ophelia.

Shylock the Jew is preached *at* by nearly all the Christians in the play for his hardness, his ungentleness, his love of gain, and mostly for his lack of mercy. And all the preachers are most potently eloquent in their condemnation of the vices he possesses, almost grandiloquent in praise of the virtue he lacks. With what a tone of assumed superiority does Antonio rail at this "Jew dog" for his *ungentle* practices, yet scruples not to spit upon him, spurn him and call him dog, and when the Jew remonstrates, says—

> "I am as like to call thee so again,
> To spit on thee again, to spurn thee too."

After this to appeal to the Jew's mercy on Antonio's behalf, as though that *gentleman* had never wronged him, is rank hypocrisy.

In the whole of the trial scene, which is a masterpiece of dramatic skill, Shylock has the best of the argument, and not only so, but of the question at issue; and a verdict for him only fails through a legal flaw. The verdict having gone against "the dog," the Duke, who sits in judgment, thus shows his mercy, to demonstrate, as he puts it, "the difference of our spirit"—he takes all his worldly goods. The Jew's argument: "Take my life and all, pardon not that; you take my house when you do take the prop that doth sustain my house; you take my life when you do take the means whereby I live," goes for nothing.

So much for the Christian Duke's mercy,— the Duke who wished to show the difference in their spirits. Gratiano—the funny man of the piece, and withal a poor one—who had been very loud in protestation against this unchristian hater of pork, suggests, when Antonio is asked what mercy shall be rendered to the Jew—

"A halter gratis; nothing else, for God's sake."

Mark the "for God's sake," since Gratiano had been gushing and vehement in praise of Portia's definition of mercy—mercy, an attribute of God himself; a beautiful thing in theory, thought Gratiano; "a halter gratis" was his practice of it.

Antonio can think of no more gracious act than that the victim be allowed to render unto him one-half his goods in use, to revert upon the old man's death to "the gentleman that lately *stole* his daughter, and that for this favour he presently became a Christian." One and all, directly or indirectly affected by this trial, do the same thing. When they stood in fear of the man, when they had something to gain, they told him what were good to be done; when Fortune reversed the conditions, not one out of the twenty could follow his own teaching.

And so, again, in *Hamlet*. This wordy philosopher preaches to himself and to all who come within his hearing of what ought to be done, and never does one good action. Fortinbras, who, I take it, is purposely designed by Shakspere as a contrast and foil to Hamlet, is a man of action, and takes the crown that Hamlet loses.

And so we play our parts to-day. We all want to preach, teach and direct,—it is so easy, seems so gracious, and weaves, as it were, for each individual preacher a garment to hide his own shortcomings. And this in the main is true, the best teachers are the worst performers, be they writers or orators. The most eloquent preacher to whom I have listened, proved himself to be one of the blackest sheep in the congregation; the man that condemned drunkenness more than any man I have known, was the greatest drunkard himself it has been my misfortune to meet; the most persistent gambler with whom I am acquainted gives the best advice on the folly of gaming to be obtained; the most strait-laced schoolmistress, —and, for the matter of that, as a moral teacher, the best I could recommend,—has two children born out of wedlock; and, lastly, a near neighbour of mine is everlastingly quoting that patience is a virtue, and he is the most impatient fiend that ever tyrannized over a gentle wife.

"It is a good divine that follows his own instructions," says our text-giver. Yes, and a rare one. I doubt if any more sensible lines than those put into the mouth of Portia, in the second scene of the first act of *The Merchant of Venice*, have ever been written. I have given but five instances of mortals who failed to practice what they preached. I could give more,—doubtless so could the reader,—but for practical purposes they will suffice, as, I take it, the fact is indisputable, though the reason be not obvious.

At first sight it would seem that this unpractised philosophy was a cloak to cover or excuse personal failings, but it is not always so. In the case of the clergyman and the drunkard it may have been; in the case of the gambler it was not. The parson was a talented hypocrite, who made capital out of his teaching, and, be it admitted, was but fairly remunerated for his services; for, though his aim was not honourable, the result was doubtless highly satisfactory. The gambler was as clever and as kind-hearted a man as ever drew breath in smoky London, but sadly in want of ballast. He tried not to hide his weakness, nor, I am afraid, to fight against it; still he pointed out in the clearest manner possible the shallowness of his own fascination. Of the drunkard, he was a fool, and vainly tried to hide his animalism (for I can devise no truer term for the idolater of Bacchus) by condemning the course he so chronically pursued. Of the three, strange to say, the hypocrite did the most good; and I have no hesitation in saying that, whereas he reclaimed thousands from the evil path he discoursed against, the others between them scarce reclaimed one.

From this it must not be inferred that hypocrisy is to be upheld; on the contrary, had this theological giant been earnest, he would have converted tens of thousands in place of thousands.

In this strange world we are all more or less hypocrites (it is our birth-right), from the surfeited suckling who kicks and screams for more food, envious of its hungry brother twin, to the man who carries off the woman he does not love from a host of worthier and more deeply attached admirers. Yet that surfeited infant, could it prate, would deliver a homily on the wisdom of moderating our appetites, and hold forth in praise of the axiom "live and let live." The man whose vanity led him to marry a woman for whom he had little or no love, will rail in a spirit of social piety against any man who does the same thing; or, turning cynic, protest that matrimony is a snare, that woman in her proper sphere, and at her best, is a mistake, and out of that sphere a curse.

How easy it is to preach. How earnestly the quack advertises the patent pill he would not swallow himself for double the price. How persuasively the *honest* butcher recommends the cow-steak he would not give to his pet dog or his dainty blackbird. How skilfully the 'cute solicitor recommends his client to invest his money in a shaky mortgage, and himself invests the liberal costs of the transaction in a snug little security that his legal eye has long coveted. Yes, we can all preach : the father to his son, the mother to her daughter ; and, stopping at the bottom of the hill of life ourselves, urge others to climb the bank, and point out the safest path.

And why is it? Unfortunately, our vanity prompts us all to be generals rather than rank and file, as becomes our station and our experience ; the poet with his puny rhymes, the bigot with his sickly tracts,—in short, as long as we can reach heaven with a string of goodly converts in our wake to appease the anger of a just God at our own personal misconduct, we vainly imagine we shall be rewarded for the good teaching we have ingrafted into others, though we ourselves have discarded the dictates of our faith, and followed the butterfly flight of our animal inclinations.

As the miserly tailor turns out a coat for a king, and struts about himself in a bilious garment that a missionary would not recommend to a savage chieftain, so the priest, the drunkard, the gambler, the straight-laced schoolmistress and the impatient man, tendered the excellent advice they did not personally follow.

Charity should begin at home, as the reproving wife said to the reckless husband who generously offered the cold leg of mutton to the passing beggar. Reformation, like Charity, should begin at home; and it would be far wiser for us all to look to the mending of our own shoes ere we go out of our way to point out the holes in our friend's boots; better to secure a fair competency for ourselves ere we strive to help our less fortunate companions with the product of our industry.

True, it is far more pleasant to be the architect of a building, to watch the bricks laid one by one by the weary labourer in the broiling sun, whilst we smoke our cigar and drink our brandy and soda in the shady foundations; but we are not all eligible for the post, and the discontented labourer who undertakes the architecture of a building would in all probability find his would-be mansion an elevated hovel.

Let us look to ourselves, and if we can honestly convince our reason we are clean, then by all means set about the pleasing task of washing our uncleanly brethren; for though I do not say the dirty nigger at the Turkish bath is not capable of thoroughly cleansing his master's feverish customers, yet I feel assured that the worthy establishment would be more patronized if these dusky servants took a greater interest in the welfare of their own skins. In fact, though good may come out of evil, better will surely come out of good. Mere words are breath, and as vapour disappear. Action is the fruit that feeds and still bears seed. So the noisy leaves of the full-blown tree harmoniously murmur of unknown good in the summer breeze, then fade and die and leave no mark, whilst the silent root works to drain the soil of its goodness, and become the source of the visible life.

Essay XIV.

DRUNKENNESS.

"O, that men should put an enemy in their mouths to steal away their brains! that we should, with joy, pleasance, revel, and applause, transform ourselves into beasts."

. . . . . .

"Is your Englishman so expert in his drinking?"
"Why, he drinks you, with facility, your Dane dead drunk; he sweats not to overthrow your Almain; he gives your Hollander a vomit, ere the next pottle can be filled."—*Othello*, Act ii. sc. 3.

IT is essential in dealing with this subject that I should first of all give a few facts. Facts and statistics are dry reading, but when duly considered and pondered over, speak more eloquently than many flowers of rhetoric;—rhetoric, at the best, is but a spring daisy, facts are evergreens. Within a few years—namely, fifteen—the police statistics show that drunkenness has increased 247 per cent., and is gradually increasing. The number of persons upon whom a coroner's inquest returned a verdict of "died from excessive drinking" was, in 1875, 516. The consumption of wine and spirits has gone up, since 1861 to 1875, from 35 millions of gallons to $59\frac{1}{4}$ millions of gallons; malt used for brewing, during the same period, has gone up from 46 millions of bushels to 63 millions of bushels.

Drunkenness was, no doubt, very prevalent in Shakspere's time; for, apart from other evidence, we find Sir Matthew Hale, Chief

Justice of England, declaring, some fifty years after the poet's death, that if the enormities committed for the space of the last twenty years of his administration were divided into five parts, four of them would be found to be the issues and product of excessive drinking.*

Nearer to, and in our own time, no less than 23 English Judges (than whom there are no class of men less given to exaggeration) confirm this appalling truth ; drunkenness, they say, is at the root of nine-tenths of the crimes committed in this country.†
The population of London is one-third greater than that of Lancashire, yet the number of

---

* *Crime in England and Wales.* William Hoyle.
† *Ibid.*

persons brought before the magistrates is 34 per cent. greater in Lancashire than in London. Does any one care to know the reason? Lancashire has 16,272 Public Hells, licensed by Christian magistrates, in a Christian country, for the profit and benefit of the Devil and his agents. London has *only* 9,709; hence there are not quite so many in the capital of *civilised* England who " tread the primrose way to the everlasting bonfire."

Mr Chamberlain says, in his able speech made in the House of Commons on 13th March 1877, that " the English people are becoming impatient of the continual existence of intemperance, which is the plague-spot of our civilisation; that they are determined to grapple in some way or other with the evil which is the bane of our national life, which poisons the source of our national satisfaction in times of prosperity, and which in times of adversity adds fresh bitterness to our calamities."

Truly it is high time we did grapple with this evil,—this evil that taints all our one-sided virtues,—this sieve through which every goodness is filtered. Our workhouses are full of paupers, whose lives are burdens to themselves, whose existence is a burden to the ratepayers ; 50 per cent. of our lunatics are men and women whose brains have been floated, so to speak, in a sea of noxious adulterations ; our idiot asylums are full of the children of drunken parents—children begotten in sin and semi-idiotcy ; our gaols are full to overflowing with savage animals called men, who have excelled in swinish gluttony the very swine we contemn; our scaffold-boards are trod, in ninety-nine cases of the hundred, by murderers made so by the influence of the great social poison; and our national family skeleton, from palace to hovel, is a tippler. It is this devil in the shape of drink that keeps the street-walker to her trade, hardens her heart, softens her brain, and drowns at last all her better feelings, all womanly instincts, all traces even of her claim to nobler humanity. It is destroying our physical strength as a nation; it is weakening our intellectual growth, diluting our minds, sapping our energies, warring against our sense of right and wrong, and sweeping our very souls into a powerful current whose goal is everlasting death.

Let us hang one or two companion-pictures in our National Gallery. They will not be so pleasant to look upon, may-be, as Landseer's animals, but they may help to show us what animals *we* are.

A fresh green lane in summer time, a youthful, hopeful pair, betrothed by every sacred vow to make each other happy. The young man is strong-built, ruddy and handsome, with manly health and vigour; the woman is no less ruddy, and even pretty for her class of life. The sun sinking in the horizon, or the lamps of heaven glowing brightly are poetic mysteries to them, but they infuse their untutored minds with awe and reverence, and in their simple way they deem the shining host to be the approving eyes of angels looking down upon their love, and the glittering silver dew upon the flowers the reflected smiles of seraphim.

Turn we now to the companion picture: The framework, or blank canvas, which separates the two, aptly conveys the little time that has elapsed to change one of those summer lovers into a mindless, soulless, inhuman sot. The once ruddy, buxom, peasant girl is pale and thin. The furrows in her cheeks have not been traced by the kindly hand of Time, but rudely tribulated by many bitter tears, wept in vain, and lost, utterly lost, in the great ocean of human woe. There is a baby at her breast, imbibing the sustenance she can so ill-afford to give. The last flicker of unsavoury grease is dying out; the last ember of a cheerless fire is throwing its weird shadows on the damp-stained wall, and illumines the grim darkness as with an evil eye; there are no stars in heaven now, for there there is economy, and "the candles are all out;" the flowers are faded all; aye, and worse, she has discovered the serpent underneath. The silence is a twin to the darkness, and is only broken now and then by the woman's painful sighs, or the distant murmur of rude, rough voices. Suddenly, loudly the door opens, and the husband staggers in with a fierce or filthy oath upon his lips—lips swollen and thickly black with vitriol and nicotine. There is violence and mischief in the clenching of his hands; there is murder, foul and unnatural, in the wild glare of his eyes—eyes once the mirror of God's great gift to the soul, now the devil's lantern in search of opportunity for sin. He has put the poison in his mouth, and his carcase is mere animated rottenness; he is poisoned from head to foot; his mind is a black confusion of idiotic dreams and fiendish visions; every sense, every faculty is suffused with the poison; and when he dies, the Creator he has so injured through His creatures, so insulted through himself, shall snuff out for ever his graceless and ungrateful soul.

Another picture—they could be drawn by the thousand: A happy father and mother in the middle class of life, and a bright-faced, curly-headed darling on the mother's lap. The parents are building castles in the air; their little one, their heir, the pride of their younger years, the hope of their age, what shall they make of him? Shall he be a sailor, a pretty, many-buttoned middy, and sail all over the mighty ocean, and see many sights and many countries, and grow up to be a great Captain or a grand Admiral? Or shall he be a soldier, and wear a beautiful uniform; make all the ladies fall in love with him; go to wars and fight for Queen and country, and return home a hero covered with glory? It is a pretty picture; the father's eyes grow bright with pride and pleasure, as some memories of the past are stirred within him; the mother's eyes become dim as some vague, prophetic fears for the future move her tender bosom.

The bright-faced, curly-headed darling went into the navy. Oh, how the father strove to suppress his pride and emotion when he bade farewell to his boy; how the mother's heart leapt with joy and pleasure when he returned home in his bright blue jacket and golden buttons.

A few years later, and we have the companion-picture. The "old people" are grey-haired and feeble. The old man holds a letter in his hand, which tells how his son has been court-martialed and dismissed Her Majesty's service with disgrace for drunkenness; his hand shakes as it holds the fatal letter; his voice quivers as he reads the dreaded sentence; and the mother, as she listens, buries her poor wrinkled face in her trembling hands, and feels that her heart is broken.

They are dead now, that feeble, grey-haired couple; their bodies lie peacefully in the village churchyard, and their souls, God grant, united in one of his glorious mansions. But the bright-faced, curly-headed darling? I met him the other day; he was being turned out of a tavern, "beastly drunk." The once bright face is blotched and pimpled; the hair is unkempt and almost straight; those "sweet blue eyes," his mother's special pride, are glazed and blood-shot, and reflect his ruling passions—debauchery and sensuality. He married a prostitute and had children; but *she* left him for a less drunken scoundrel, and *they* died of the scrofula and vitriol that was born in them. He goes on drinking, and, whether drunk or sober, is a sight to make the angels weep and some men pray.

What is the staple argument of those who protest against legislation that shall effectually stamp out our national vice? Liberty of the subject,—freedom for the base and depraved majority to overrule, to overtax, to scandalize a less base but a weak-minded minority,—liberty in favour of nine drunkards to the detriment of the one sober man. Liberty of the subject forsooth! Liberty for the subject to put a poison in his mouth to steal away his brains !—liberty for the impecunious scoundrel to drink enough to give him courage to rob!—liberty for the black-hearted to nerve himself to murder!—liberty for the inordinate sensualist to deflower the innocent!—liberty, in short, for the baser subject to make himself a slave to crime!

When so much is said and so much is written of our boasted civilisation, how superior we are in every way to our neighbours,—our advanced intellect leaving Germany in the rear, our improved sciences leaving France but a poor second, our perfect poor laws (God save the mark!), our sanitary arrangements, leaving such semi-barbarous countries as Spain, Portugal, and Italy nowhere in the race,—I confess it is with a sneer I am inclined to ask if Germany, France, Spain, Portugal, and Italy combined could produce so many human swine as *civilised* England? When so much is said, so much written, and such horror and indignation shown anent the Turkish atrocities, it is with shuddering contempt I am forced to demand, if leaving the bodies of slaughtered victims to rot in the sun be a worse crime than allowing one's own young to starve, and then, in a paroxysm of drunken fury, throwing the corpse at the bereaved and sorrowful mother?—if killing with sword and bayonet the wives and children of foes be more brutal than kicking to death a defenceless and *enceinte* woman?—if the ravishing of sundry Christian maidens by Turks in Bulgaria or elsewhere be more shocking, more repulsive, than the criminal assaults committed by a semi-drunken father upon his own three daughters, the youngest of whom was eleven?

When so much is said and so much written about our reformed Protestant religion and our regenerated morality, I confess it is with shame and sorrow I am fain to ask, if the worship of the bottle be less pernicious than the worship (be it real or supposed) of gaudy images?—if our protests against a debased and superstitious ritual be more powerful in virtue's cause than is our permission of "the inordinate cup"?—if our disclaimer of the "real presence" be more . potent for good than is our sanction for the consumption of Devil's blood?

Essay XV.

LOVE.

"Love is blind."
   Two Gentlemen of Verona, Act ii. sc. 1.

"Love is blind, and lovers cannot see
 The pretty follies that themselves commit."
   Merchant of Venice, Act. ii. sc. 6.

"Love is merely a madness; and deserves as well a dark house and a whip, as madmen do.
   As You Like It, Act iii. sc. 3.

"There lives within the very flame of love
 A kind of wick or snuff that will abate it;
 And nothing is at a like goodness still;
 For goodness, growing to a pleurisy,
 Dies in his own too much.
   Hamlet, Act iv. sc. 7.

> "Thou blind fool, Love, what dost thou to mine eyes,
> That they behold and see not what they see?
> *Sonnet*, 137.

OF the many thousand subjects upon which Shakspere has dilated, there is, *of course*, not one that claimed more of his attention than the subject—Love. We can cull on an average about fifty pertinent and more or less sapient remarks on every subject which he touched; of Love we have at least four hundred. I say *of course* there is no other subject upon which he dilated so fully, because Shakspere, like all poets and dramatists, was obliged to build his works on that eternal foundation, because the theme of Love is the only one, for the large majority of men and women, that never grows stale,—the only theme of real interest to youth,—the only theme that creates in the old an interest in the young. Without Love there would be no poetry worth reading, no plays worth the seeing. It is pre-eminently *the* one emotion of the human heart,—the sun to which all other emotions are but planets.

Apart from Shakspere's universal genius, which gives him an absolute right to opinion, we have the fact that he himself loved and married the object of his attachment. And none can doubt that he loved with all the ardour of his passionate youth (he was but eighteen when he married), with all the intensity of his glowing imagination, and with all the fervour of his poetic temperament. His youth had not been contaminated by association with the bad and evil of either sex; his pure imagination had not been sullied, like Lord Byron's, by a precocious knowledge; nor had his poetic temperament suffered any check that could make it more practical and worldly-wise. On this ground, therefore, if no other existed, he has a right to speak with the voice of authority.

To follow Shakspere's mind, therefore, as that mind developed,—to trace through his works, in the order of their creation, his views on this mighty theme of Love,—to watch the gradual change in his estimate of the grand passion as his mental vision becomes more and more clear, as the sentimental and romantic, while never wholly taking their exit, yet left room upon the vast stage of his intellect for reason to be seen and heard, is surely a task at once of great interest and instruction.

According to Malone, *The Two Gentlemen of Verona* was Shakspere's first play, and this comedy was succeeded by *Midsummer Night's Dream* and *Romeo and Juliet*. These then are our poet's earliest productions, and they are love poems. From these three plays we get the greatest number of tender, passionate, and sentimental passages. From these plays I could quote nearly all the gushing love rhapsodies of which Shakspere (if I may be allowed to say so) has been guilty. It is in these plays that the blind, wayward little god has full scope, and the heroes and heroines give vent to that sweet, mad, beatiful, inane, poetical rubbish common to all lovers in every age.

After these plays our bard becomes a little more practical; his heroes and heroines love just as fervently, but a little more sensibly, until we get to *Othello*, when married love is dealt with, and a married man, namely, Iago, a man devoid of all romance, but full of worldly philosophy, puts Love in a corner, for he defines it. He gives the source of this ever flowing river. It is not a pleasant source; it is not romantic, nor beautiful, nor poetic; and the ocean into which it tends, though large, is not mighty, nor grand, nor majestic. The source of the river is passion, and the ocean into which it flows, and in which it is lost, gratification.

"I take this that you call love to be merely a lust of the blood, and a permission of the will."

One of the oddest things in human nature is its blindness, its willing blindness,—a preference for darkness in certain instances instead of light, a selecting of falsehood in place of truth, because darkness and falsehood hide the skeleton we are so afraid to look upon. But light and truth are inseparable twins, and, play the ostrich as we may, they will find us out.

We may contemn, we may deny, we may grow indignant when put face to face with truth, but the light must in the end dazzle us, and we drop our eyes, for truth must stare us out of countenance. "It is merely a lust of the blood, a permission of the will." Do we demand proof? We all know in what sense the words "lust of the blood" is used. Take away this lust of the blood, then, and where is the Love? Where is this charming, romantic, sentimental, poetical Love? Take away the source, and the river ceases to flow. Analyse the dead body, let the senses take fright, and the romantic in our nature will wear a curb ever after.

"To the pure all things are pure," doubtless, and in all the functions of nature there is nothing that should disgust a healthy mind; but nevertheless no logical mind, however healthy, will allow for any length of time a halo of romance and poetry to be thrown around any one of nature's functions. But the young couple, madly in love one with the other, never seek to find the origin of their love,—they love, that is enough. For the passion which is the cause is dormant,—so fast asleep, in fact, that they regard it as a thing that is dead. In the man, however, his love, though it be his first, is seldom, if ever, the sweet, divine mystery, that it is to the woman. For him, knowledge has blunted the keen edge of anticipation; for her, ignorance will elevate the real to an ideal she will never live to know.

Truly with man "love is a thing apart." He does not believe it to be so when he first loves. Unwittingly he guages his love by his passion ; he cannot foresee the possibility that after marriage his passion may be less though his real affection may be more ; he cannot, in the salad days of his first love, grasp the fact that a man can be surfeited with honey,—that he can leave " a celestial bed to feed on garbage "—because as yet his mouth only waters for the honey to come, in profound ignorance of the time that cometh, when the mouth, over full with honey, satiated unto nausea with sweet-stuff, will seek a change of diet, or prefer starvation.

"Nothing is at a like goodness still." The first passionate, romantic, poetic love of man must, when the passion by gratification has abated, lose the first blush of its romance and poetry. The scales fall from his eyes; he begins to love what he does see, not what he thought he saw; his two eyes are wide open, and with one eye at least he can discover faults.

With the woman it is otherwise. She loves unto the end, more or less blindly. A young girl, pure, good, and trusting, gives herself absolutely and without reserve to the man she loves. She asks of him no account of his past life; she only desires that to her, and to her alone, shall belong the present and the future. She craves a fidelity from him equal to her own—a love as absolute as her own. In her sweet innocence, her womanly goodness, her simple trust, she can entertain no other idea. For her familiarity can breed no contempt,—nay, it cannot breed indifference. From her the halo of romantic, poetic love never wholly departs; and even when her passion is quite dead,—and it dies by inches as every child is born to her,—she realises what it may be still to him, and in lieu of the old faith, "myself and my pleasure first," embraces a less selfish creed.

Yet with all this difference between the love of the man and the love of the woman after marriage, it is strange, though true, that the man is capable of a greater sacrifice for the woman than she for the man. For her well-being, for her greater happiness, should emergency arise, he would sacrifice all, —ambition, fortune, status, children, everything. She will go all the way with him till the last step,—at the children she halts. There are few wives, if any, who are mothers, who would not sacrifice the husband for the child,—aye, though the husband be the best man ever moulded out of clay, and the child the most ill-conditioned, wayward, ungrateful, ugly brat ever born to make a bad world worse. And when she has no child of her own, she will sometimes learn to love the child of another,—and love it, too, better than she does her husband, even as Paulina loved Perdita better than she loved Antigonus, though he was no bad husband, and she had borne him children. For the sweet, helpless, unfortunate baby all her full heart of sympathy is stirred ; for the tender, graceful, lovely girl restored to her mother all her full heart of joy is exercised. For the husband, the good father of her own children, she sheds but one crocodile tear, and when the reaction after great joy begins to set in, she exclaims :

> " I, an old turtle,
> Will wing me to some wither'd bough ; and there
> My mate, that's never to be found again,
> Lament till I am lost."

It is sweetly pretty, and touching in the extreme. "I, an old turtle." The allusion to the dove, the emblem of pure, constant love, is most happy,—for her mate that's never to be found she will lament till she is lost. And yet the very next instant doth she permit the king to bestow her hand in marriage on Camillo.

In dealing with married love Shakspere, ever true to nature, gives it no rhapsodies, or flowers of pretty speech. It may be a love that overwhelms the man's whole nature, as with Othello, when he exclaims, folding his wife to his heart, after an enforced absence which had robbed him of half his honeymoon,—

"If it were now to die, t'were now to be most happy."

Truly his love is not without its philosophy. Or Brutus, comforting his wife when she desires to know the secret that oppresses him. She has said, and said truly,

"Am I yourself,
But, as it were, in sort or limitation,—
To keep with you at meals; comfort your bed,

And talk to you sometimes? Dwell I but in the
 suburbs
Of your good pleasure? If it be no more,
Portia is Brutus' harlot, not his wife."

And his answer is full of profound, earnest, sad truth:

" You are my true and honourable wife ;
 As dear to me as are the ruddy drops
 That visit my sad heart."

Here is true, consistent, reasonable love. It does not worship the ground she walks on; it does not desire to kiss the glove she wears. He, the husband-lover, despises the ground, would throw the old glove in the fire. But Othello in that moment of joy would willingly die; for his wife would Brutus give his life. This love in the married is real; it has grown out of companionship and friendship; and passion only plays a super's part, speaks his line and departs. But the deepness and intensity of this love is rarely visible; secure in itself, it sleeps; only great accident can arouse it; for, as a modern poet sings,—*

> " The strongest love may fall on sleep,
>   But hate will waken ever,
> Strong love its full content may keep
> Within the soul so warm and deep,
>   Close-wrapped and doubting never,
> That, lost in the strength of sure delight,
> It hardly shall know of its own true being.
> .   .   .   .   .
> Sleeping in safety, nor fearing harm,
> But living to waken alive and warm,
> At kiss of the sun or clang of the storm.

It is notable that though Shakspere puts into the mouth of his heroes and heroines many splendid speeches touching on love, he never allows a lover, male or female, to define

---

* *Bjorn and Bera*, by B. Montgomerie Ranking.

it. All definition of the mysterious emotion comes either from the mouth of a married man, or a Mercutio who never loved, or an Adonis who could not love. The first defines it, as we have already noted, "a mere lust of the blood;" the second treats it with ridicule: "This drivelling love is like a great natural, that runs lolling up and down to hide his bauble in a hole;" the third, in all seriousness, exclaims:

> "Call it not love, for love to heaven is fled,
> Since sweating lust on earth usurp'd his name."

Herein lies the whole truth of the matter, what we call love as between the sexes is simply natural, healthy lust, exalted by fervid imagination into an ethereal, mysterious something that for the time being renders the lover blind. He or she cannot see the physical charms or want of them in the beloved as other men and women see them.

> "The lunatic, the lover, and the poet,
> Are of imagination all compact:
> One sees more devils than vast hell can hold—
> . . . the lover, all as frantic,
> Sees Helen's beauty in a brow of Egypt.

Nor can they, when the fit is on them, perceive the deficiency of goodness or intelligence that may exist.

> "Things base and vile, holding no quantity,
> Love can transpose to form and dignity.

Love cannot see the mere bones beneath the skin of beauty, any more than it can perceive the half hidden or dormant failings of the beloved. But to the philosopher or thinker Shakspere is a human microscope; by his aid we can look through the skin and penetrate the heart. Knowledge is power, but power is not always happiness; and happiness, after all, has in it a more godlike element than knowledge.

It is well that lovers cannot see through the skin nor penetrate the heart. There is little enough of happiness in this world, and the greatest amount of happiness for men and women exists in this sweet delusion—Love. Let us hide the skeleton in the closet, where there are many more, and be happy in our ignorance. Love! who would not be in love? It is the quintessence of mental and physical pleasure. The heart beats as it never beat before; the blood circulates as it never will again, save in fever or in madness; the joy, the happiness, the ecstasy of two lovers may not be the pleasures they have experienced, so much as the pleasures to which they look forward. At the unknown, untried source of promised joy, the lover has slaked his thirst, and the draught has made him drunk. Yet who among the lovers who have been drunk and have slept it off would awake him ere it is time? Lovers are more to be pitied than any creatures on the face of God's earth. They invest their all in an unlimited company that is doomed to bankruptcy. Even as you pity the blind man, so must you pity the lover; even as you are tender and compassionate to the madman, so must you condole the idiotcy of the man or woman in love. You have been blind,—remember it! You have been mad,—can you ever forget it?

Essay XVI.

HYPOCRISY.

Glo. "Come, cousin, canst thou quake and change thy
  colour,
  Murder thy breath in middle of a word,
  And then again begin, and stop again,
  As if thou wert distraught, and mad with terror?"
Buck. "Tut, I can counterfeit the deep tragedian;
  Speak and look back, and pry on every side,
  Tremble and start at wagging of a straw,
  Intending deep suspicion : ghastly looks
  Are at my service, like enforc'd smiles ;
  And both are ready in their offices
  At any time to grace my stratagems."
          Richard III., Act iii. sc. 5.

THE play of *Richard III.* is, as some great critic remarks, a thorough stage play, and belongs more to the theatre than to the study. The fact is, this play gives more scope for acting than any other play by Shakspere. Richard III. is the character in which Garrick came out, the one in which the elder Kean acquired his fame ; Young, Cooke and Kemble made their greatest hits in it ; and in our own day it is thought by those who have a right to influence public opinion, that Irving's conception of Gloucester is superior to anything he has yet done. And why? Because of the scope for acting. To play well the part of a villain and a hypocrite comes naturally to all men, for the simple reason that all men play the part, more or less pronounced, every day of their lives.

It is for this reason that the villain of a piece is invariably, when in the hands of a tolerable artist, the best acted character in the entire cast. The applause given to the virtuous hero is simply called forth by the homage that vice pays to virtue; the hisses, which are the best applause, showered upon the villain arise from the realistic exactness with which the actor has delineated human nature; all perceive in it a reflex, may be an exaggerated one, of themselves.

So well does the individual who enacts the part of Judas Iscariot, in the sacred play performed every Easter in Mexico, convey to his superstitious and semi-barbarous audience the pretended goodness, the cant, the treachery and hypocrisy of this red-headed villain, that the *police* have some difficulty in preventing the enraged audience from tearing him to pieces. The hero—the God-man—is a tame performance, the actor having to struggle with a condition of mental and moral being with which he has no personal knowledge.

Again, in the early stage of English drama, when the plays were all, more or less, a representation of sacred events, the part of his Satanic Majesty was the one that stamped the performance, gave it tone, and secured the attention of the audience.

It is only on the stage that men play the villain proper; off the boards the worst villains play the proper hero. The religious cloak, as we all know, hides more vice and crime than any other; the fabled cloak of the *Arabian Nights*, which made the wearer invisible, was not more potent than is the cloak religious. Your confessed thief is less wicked than your professed saint; "give thanks to thieves professed, that they work not in holier shapes, for there is boundless theft in limited professions."

When our author tells us by the mouth of *Jacques* that "All the world's a stage, and all the men and women merely players," I take the word *players* to mean actors. We all act a part; and if our professional actors would only play the parts allotted to them on the stage by the dramatist as well as they play their parts in life's drama at home, abroad, in society, in church, in business, the critic's occupation would be gone.

Oh, how well we act our parts in life! How we smile when we want to frown; how we frown when we want to laugh; how virtuous, how indignant we are at the recital of vice; how glad, how delighted to hear of virtue's victory. Remove the mask,—for life is one grand *bal masque;* see the frown at vice turned to a boisterous laugh at the recital of a coarse joke culled from the cesspool of City brains; behold how we poohpooh at virtue, ridicule religion, condemn all sentiment, and revel generally in our natural wickedness!

Contemplate lovers, male and female. How amiable, how romantic, how agreeable, —the male never bullies the female, the female never talks *at* the male. Remove the mask;—they are married, the honeymoon is over; the amiable are fretful, the romantic are practical, the agreeable are fault-finding, the husband swears at the wife, the wife nags at the husband. They are simply natural, and off the stage.

Contemplate the *roué* at a ball or a dinner party—all politeness, all suavity, a respectful admirer of beauty, a worshipper of female chastity. Later on he is in the Haymarket with the mask off; he is drinking champagne with an "unfortunate," taking a cigar from her polluted lips, listening with eagerness to her last tale of the old lover, and, in a word, playing his part off the stage.

Behold that poor-looking, half-starved, ragged woman, in one of our most frequented thoroughfares. Poor thing! poor thing! think many of the charitable-minded, but busy folks, as they pass her by. Suddenly she leans against a shop, her face begins to work with fearful contortions, dilating of the nostrils, upturning of the eyes, down-drawing of the mouth, from which issues a frothy saliva; the hands shake, the body quivers—ha! she falls in the throes of some dreadful fit. Her rags and tatters, her thin pinched face and haggard looks are intensified as she lies upon the ground, and many think she will die. There is a large crowd around her now; one brings water, another smacks her hands, and an old lady wipes her brow with her scented kerchief. As the poor creature gradually recovers, and in a faint voice, in answer to kind enquiries, says, "She is better now, thank you; she will go her way home alone;" then with a sickly smile, in answer to the question, "Does she need help?" "Thank you, no; she is better, stronger now." Deep into his pocket goes the hand of a modern Pickwick, and he hands the *poor creature* a half-crown; some others follow suit; two or three shillings, twice as many sixpences, coppers not a few from very poor folk, and the woman who had the fit departs with a sum of money that would put to shame many a collection for a charitable purpose in some country church.

That *poor creature,* battered and torn, weary and worn, has a fit once a day, sometimes twice, in one or other of our densely thronged streets, and makes by it a larger income (the publican could tell you how much better than I) than many a poor lady slaving at her needle from early morn till late at night, or well-born, well-bred, educated governess, living in a rich family and drawing her eighty or hundred pounds a year. That *poor creature* is an actress; she is seldom off the stage, except you meet her at home, where she is but seldom, or in the bar of a Drury Lane public, where she is often.

"It is a bad world, my masters," and we continue to make it so as long as we wear our hats so pulled down over the brow that the truth in our lives cannot be read. What actors we are? The semi-bankrupt, full of smiles, treating his creditor to a glass of sherry with his last shilling, and walking home because he cannot pay his bus fare. The prosperous man, coining money with a face full of woe: "Business? there is no business now, Sir; country's going to the dogs!" He goes home in a hansom, gives the cabman his exact fare, and drinks the best sherry that can be had for money.

Hypocrites all, from the Sky-pilot in the

pulpit, pointing the way he never goes, to the petty tradesman in the pew, who pretends to repent the way he goes for six days, and is really only sorry he cannot go the same way on the seventh;—from the fine lady, who lies on a sofa and pretends to be ill, that she may have much sympathy, and be waited on like an Eastern princess, to the mock-blind singer in the streets, with a borrowed baby pinched into crying, that the hearts of her audience may be softened. "All the world's a stage, and all the men and women merely *actors.*" What part do you play?

Essay XVIII.

LOVE OF WEALTH.

" This yellow slave
Will knit and break religions ; bless the accurs'd ;
Make the hoar leprosy ador'd ; place thieves,
And give them title, knee, and approbation,
With senators on the bench."
Timon of Athens, Act iv. sc. 3.

" What can it not do, and undo ? "
Cymbeline, Act ii. sc. 3.

NEXT to the genius of invention must rank the genius of appreciation : it requires a poet to understand a poet. Just as Shakspere ranks among authors, so must

Hazlitt rank among critics, for he is *par excellence* the expounder of the truest poet, the wisest man, and the only uncanonical prophet the world has ever known. Hazlitt says of *Timon of Athens*, as well as I can remember, that it is the one play in which Shakspere seems to have been earnest from beginning to end,—in which he never trifles, nor goes out of his way,—in which he never relaxes his efforts, never loses sight of the unity of his design. It is as much a satire as a play, and contains some of the finest pieces of invective possible to be conceived; and, finally, that it is the only play of Shakspere in which spleen is the predominant feeling.

With all deference to the great critic, I think that here he has missed the motive, or rather, it would be safer to say, so expressed himself as to make it appear that he had missed the motive. The predominant feeling is not spleen in its broad or general sense, but spleen in a particular sense. Our author through *Timon of Athens* has a motive; that motive is to decry the undue power of wealth. So keenly does he feel the wrong, that he does not hesitate to make an artist and a poet sycophants to wealth, and by the mouth of Timon he says, even of his own fraternity, the great, the noble fraternity of authors: "The learned pate ducks to the golden fool."

As evidence of Shakspere's feeling with regard to money, let us weigh the importance of the following facts :—In thirty-seven plays and five poems we have no less than forty-one distinct invective passages on the ill use, abuse, corruption and misery engendered by money, as against two passages only in faint praise of its good. This, taken with the fact, which Rowe tells us in his *Life of Shakspere*, that the great man was indifferent to literary fame, after his first youthful vanity was gratified, and that he considered his genius and his improved skill in composition only as the means of acquiring independence for his family, and securing an early retirement from the anxieties of public life, must, I think, demonstrate the motive. Such a mind as Shakspere's could never have condescended to the scraping together of money, except for the noble purpose of saving his family and his family's name from the pain and the stain of poverty. But this necessity, no matter how great, would not lessen the bitterness to him, nor make him love the necessary evil. The noble end would not sanctify the means to him. Doubtless he felt, as most of us have felt in our better and more reflective moments, that the Scripture writer of old was right,—" Money is the root of all evil."

The radical cause from which has grown the baneful Upas, whose leaves feed and whose branches shelter all the social burrs of modern civilization, all the phases of hypocrisy that, like a black mask, hides men's hearts one from another. The necessities of life, which only gold can buy; the luxuries of an easy existence, which much gold alone can procure; the influence, the power it commands; the respect of mental and moral superiors; the civility, the cringing obedience of those beneath us that it creates, are temptations to the great and small mind alike, so great, overpowering and infatuating, that no modern bull's eye in the hands of a Diogenes would light upon a really honest man. No, not one; every man under necessity, has his price.

There is more truth than cynicism in this Walpole axiom. Your only negatively honest man is the man who has no need to be dishonest,—whose position, or possessions (by what means acquired by him, or his forefathers, who shall say?) makes the virtue easy—who finds, in fact, that honesty, as the word accepts the term, is the best policy,— not because, in a right good conscience, he thinks it so, but because he can afford the luxury.

In no mixed assembly of men will the truth of this be allowed, because in no mixed assembly will there be found one of sufficient candour, or strong moral courage, to admit the failing of mankind in this direction, lest the general admission should include himself. This is the tolerated and recognised hypocrisy that constitutes, or helps to constitute, polite society.

Let us, however, put to the test these "honourable men," the virtuous and vehement protestors against what will, no doubt, be termed a baneful theory. Every man in his heart of hearts admits the eleventh Commandment: "Thou shalt not be found out." Given, in the first place, an absolute feeling of security against detection, and, in the second place, necessity—necessity! that by misconstruction can so easily be made a virtue; then let one of the "honourable," but needy, protestors against "a baneful theory" find a bag of gold. If he be a man of good sentiment he will probably endeavour to find the owner, because he or she may be as poor, or poorer, than himself; and, this being so, he will sigh, and, perhaps, restore the treasure: but, should he learn that the loser is a Rothschild, a Timon with a hidden storehouse, who offers no reward for the recovery of the lost gold, or does offer a reward, but not sufficient in amount to cover the necessity of the finder, then will he smile pleasantly and pocket the purse, as some devil of sophistry whispers in his ear:—

> "He that is robb'd, not wanting what is stolen,
> Let him not know it, and he's not robb'd at all."

It is an unpleasant truth, no doubt; but the sooner men learn to admit it the sooner will they begin to amend, for amendment can only follow the confession. It is so easy, by vehement protestation and assumption of virtue, to deceive one's neighbour, and, far worse, one's self. The popular idol has grown to such alarming dimensions, that it can no longer be said, truly, that, "To be honest, as this world goes, is to be one man picked out of ten thousand." I fear he could not be picked out of as many millions.

Our inordinate love of money and money-making has reduced our national honesty to a mere question of expediency, that sits above conscience,—expediency, that bias of the world, "that smooth-faced gentleman, tickling commodity." There is no high-minded, soul-love of the virtue, honesty, left. And this is not all; for, while this sordid love has all but destroyed one great virtue, it has patched with vice a dozen others. We are selling our very souls for dross,—vile, contaminated, a thousand times contaminated, bits of gold and silver, for which we are bartering all noble aims, all elevating ambitions.

The glory of wealth! What is it after all? A bearing of a sin-stained burden but a journey, for death to unload us. The acquisition of money? A poison that shall warp the minds of our sons and daughters,—that shall transform, as we draw near our supreme moment, their once love-lit eyes into the glare of the vulture awaiting the fall of its prey. The love, the esteem our money purchased, will die with our departing; our names shall last no longer than the gold-consoled widow weeps, and then be relegated to the limbo of forgotten glories.

Essay XVIII.

FRIENDSHIP.

"We are born to do benefits."
  Timon of Athens, Act i. sc. 4.

"A friend should bear his friend's infirmities."
  Julius Cæsar, Act iv. sc. 3.

"What need we have any friends, if we should ne'er have need of them? They were the most needless creatures living, should we ne'er have use for them, and would most resemble sweet instruments hung up in cases, that keep their sounds to themselves."
  Timon of Athens, Act i. sc. 2.

THE texts above quoted must appeal to all with equal force—to every individual, to all classes, to all nations. It would be no difficult task to crowd these pages with quotations from Shakspere to demonstrate, if need existed, how strongly he felt in the matter of friendship, how keenly he appreciated the bond of brotherhood that should exist between man and man, irrespective of blood, of race, colour or creed. The inherent selfishness of man, his pride of birth or wealth or station, his absorption in the daily pursuits of his own well-being, his life-long endeavours to raise himself above his fellows rather than raise his fellows with himself, and, above all, his overweening conceit in his own powers, and the individual vanity that makes him contemplate with such complacency his few good points through the lens of imagination, and his many faults through the wrong end of a telescope, reversing the process when he deals with his neighbour, have combined to isolate him in the present day from the great virtue of that friendship of which one of our poets has said, it was "to men and angels only given."

And rightly said, for true friendship is the least selfish of the many loves that obtain in and exercise the human mind from infancy to age. I say the least selfish, because there is some grain of selfishness in every affection of the human heart, from the highest affection that rules our conduct with reference to our Creator, to the lowest affection that governs our actions to the dumb creatures of our keeping. Every good action, every noble impulse, every motive, can be traced to a love of self.

The "grand passion," of which every poet of every country has written, and written his best to extol and etherealize, hiding the one black spot—animal passions—with many words, diverting the attention from what it really is to the grand castle in the air wherein dwells the visionary *might be*, is of all human loves the most necessary and yet the least worthy. The source of the necessity is the origin also for the unworthiness—the selfish passions which appeal to the lower nature of man as an animal. Man, freed from the flesh, has no need of the "grand passion;" but whether in the flesh or in the spirit, his higher nature can never dispense with that love which we call friendship,—the intellectual sympathy, the inter-communion of congenial souls.

But friendship, like many another thing in this age of progress, has lost much of this vigour, because much of the self-abnegation which characterised this virtue before science had attained those glorious dimensions which turns all things but progress in materialism into ridicule. The modern progressionist would reduce friendship to a science—with some it is already an art,—and, if this cannot be done, he bids you shelve "the sweet instrument," that it may keep its sound to itself, and in a case too, lest some stray breeze call it into feeble play. The great and noble friendships between man and man, which, like sun rays, serve to relieve the black and bloody canvas of human history, become fewer and fewer, as the progress of the age teaches us the art of a greater selfishness, and invites us to laugh where once we wept, and never to weep at all. In lieu of the sun rays from heaven, we are offered the limelight of the stage. There seems to be left no room in a man's heart now—no spot wherein he can hide his friend's faults; he cannot bear a friend's infirmities, so in another sense he bares them to all the world.

In his terse, epigrammatical way, Shakspere comes at once to the very pith of the subject by the question, "What need we have any friends if we should never have need of them?" He does not imply, as the cynic would doubtless argue, that we must make use of our friends, and be careful our friends make no use of us; but he means that it is the need, the necessity, the adversity, that calls for the display of friendship; that if we have no need, then, indeed, would friendship be a mere toy, a fashionable, frivolous bauble.

The one grand need, however, which must ever be a powerful reason why man cannot exist, with any degree of happiness, without some kind of friendship, is his craving, whether in joy or grief, for sympathy. Man only finds the sympathy he desires in his brother man. A woman's sympathy, though often given when withheld by man, is but a poor and chilling substitute, not from any lack of affection, but because she wants the intellectual grasp that would enable her to perceive in what way or form to sympathise. Friendship is the highest form of human love, and is, therefore, only given to the highest of the human race—" to men and angels only given."

After the affection as between one man and another, must come the love, the feeling of brotherhood, that should link all men in the union of a united family. "We were born to do benefits;"—this should be the axiom to supplant the grossly selfish and wholly unchristian phrase so prevalent in this age of progress, of "Every man for himself, and God for us all." If every man be but for himself, be sure God will be for none. And I have marked of late that even this quasi-christian termination of "God for us all," that comes in like a "God have mercy on your soul!" after a sentence of capital punishment, is often omitted, and "Every man for himself" is passed from mouth to mouth, is enacted day by day, and, may be to the satisfaction of the materialist, is becoming a perfect science in its completeness of absolute selfishness.

The idea of brotherhood, which must of necessity embrace the Shaksperian axiom, "We are born to do benefits," seems to be confined to a few bodies or cliques of men, and does not extend, as it should, to all classes of men. Our national sense of brotherhood, which should be a broad-minded cosmopolitan charity, that knows of no religious prejudice, no political bias, no prejudgment because of caste or race or colour, has degenerated into a narrow Samaritanism that savours of the feeble charity of Exeter Hall, that would aid and then pass on the other side,—a Samaritanism that can never grasp the sense of true brotherhood conveyed in the words of our poet, " It is not enough to help the feeble up, but to support him afterwards."

The temper of true brotherhood is to overcome ill-doing by good deeds, to leave the world a little better than we found it, to have a high standard of goodness, and raise others to it ; not to look down from, may be, our high pedestal with an indifference or contempt that precludes charity, or a cynical criticism that excludes justice, but to stoop, if need be, in order to raise some fellow creature in the struggling mass below to a seat on that moral pedestal where indeed there is room for all.

We look, however, on all sides, and in vain, for that universal love that bespeaks true brotherhood. In vain we seek to find it in those who, in the abstract, are united by a common Christianity; for every form, every sect, every particular shade of followers of divine doctrine, damns with every prayer it utters the brother who cannot see through the same spectacles. In vain we turn to the fraternity of letters—a fraternity only in name: it knows no charity; it perverts justice, and loves only a lynch-law; it breakfasts on prejudgment, dines on malice, and retires with the down-going of the sun with bitterest hatred.

In fine, every special fraternity nurses the notion that each member in it is a member of his own household, and consequently, not to belie the prophet, his own foe. Yet each man knows in his heart that the Great Architect of the Universe loves the work of His own hand; and in leaving man to complete the design, calls upon him, by direct command and by a thousand indirect influences, to labour in love, to hold together, "and learn the wisdom of universal love, the true self-interest of strict brotherhood."

THE NEW
SHAKSPERIAN DICTIONARY OF QUOTATIONS
By G. SOMERS BELLAMY.

OPINIONS OF THE PRESS.

"The task which Mr Bellamy has undertaken, and on which he has bestowed considerable pains, is not so easy as would at first sight appear. The quotations given are very numerous, and the text from which they are taken appears to be sound. The addition of an index renders it a most valuable contribution to this species of literature."—*Spectator*, September 30, 1876.

"Mr Bellamy's Dictionary differs from other works of the kind in giving a classification of ideas. . . . . The work is executed with judgment and taste."—*The Saturday Review*, July 10.

"To collect the thoughts on so many subjects of so keen and quick a thinker as Shakspere is surely work worth doing, and, as a rule, this work is well done."—*The Athenæum*, July 10.

"FLIRTATION:"
A COMEDY IN THREE ACTS.

BY
G. SOMERS BELLAMY AND FREDERICK ROMER.

First produced at "The Globe," 14th July 1877, and reproduced 20th May 1878.

OPINIONS OF THE PRESS.

"'Flirtation,' by Messrs Bellamy and Romer, still keeps its position in the play-bill, and enables Mr Righton, as the amatory old fop Major Shoreshot, to continue amusing the audience by a highly humorous performance."—*Daily Telegraph*.

"'Tis a mirth-moving comedy that afforded me more amusement than 'Our Boys' itself; and this I say in spite of the fact that 'Our Boys' has run over 800 nights. Why, 'Flirtation' overflows with fun and humour, character and point. There was a Robertsonian touch about the dialogue that was especially refreshing and de-

OPINIONS OF THE PRESS—*Continued.*

lightful. Mr Righton's Major Shoreshot ought to be ere long the talk of town, for it is certainly worthy of being ranked with the famous Major of Mr J. S. Clarke. As for Miss Lydia Foote, she was bright, laughter-loving, sweetly human, pathetic—all that was bright and fascinating."—*Illustrated News.*

"In the comedy 'Flirtation,' Mr Righton resumes his old part of Major Shoreshot, one of the most genuinely funny pieces of acting he has yet given us."—*Standard.*

"To the authors of this piece we can conscientiously give high praise. They have produced a play whose sole imperfection is a slight want of knowledge of stage effect, a thing that only experience can give ; and we shall look with interest for the next work of these promising young dramatists. Mr Righton has never had a part better suited to him than Major Shoreshot ; but without doubt the palm of praise belongs to Miss Lydia Foote. In this play she is nothing but smiles, and is perfect."—*Weekly Dispatch.*

"In the comedy of 'Flirtation,' Mr Righton resumes his original part of Major Shoreshot. Nothing could be better in its way than his representation. The entertainment is wholly to the taste of a large section of playgoers."—*Globe.*

"During this season two really good comedies by new authors have been brought to light at *matinée* performances ; the first was Mr Sydney Grundy's 'Mammon ;' the second is 'Flirtation,' a light, but sparkling comedy by Messrs Bellamy and Romer."—*Sporting and Dramatic News.*

TWO WEDDING RINGS:
A NOVEL.

By G. SOMERS BELLAMY,

Author of "The New Shaksperian Dictionary of Quotations."

OPINIONS OF THE PRESS.

"There is evidence of painstaking, and a pleasant fancy."—*Spectator,* June 24.

"Mr Bellamy's plot is bold and ingenious, and shows him to be possessed of real dramatic construction."—*Graphic,* October 28.

"Essentially dramatic in its interest. The author's strong point is evidently the construction of a plot with plenty of stirring incident. Mr Bellamy's English does credit to his studies of our earlier writers, and dialogue displays him at his best."—*Morning Post,* November 1.

www.ingramcontent.com/pod-product-compliance
Lightning Source LLC
Chambersburg PA
CBHW031750230426
43669CB00007B/561